AF265552

The Family of Mr. D. leaving for a milder climate. Chap 8d.

THE RED LION;

OR,

Home in Humble Life.

NORTHAMPTON:

BRIDGMAN AND CHILDS.

BOSTON: FOR SALE BY THE MASS. S. S. SOCIETY.

1865.

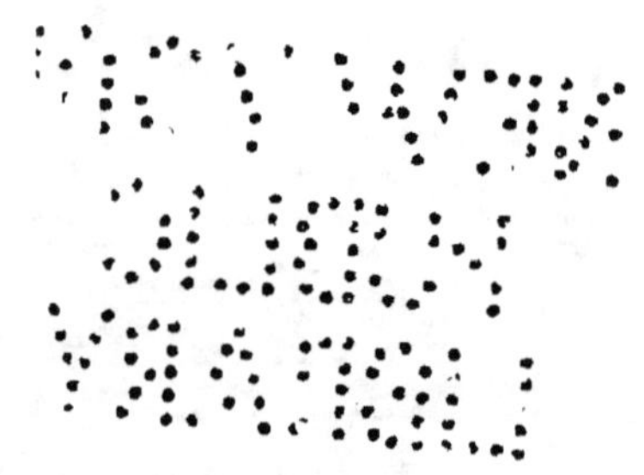

CAMBRIDGE PRESS:
DAKIN AND METCALF.

CONTENTS.

THE RED LION.

I.

Temptation; how to Resist it.

THE " Red Lion " was once a respectable, quiet public-house, in its way, but had been converted into a " palace." Its master was bent on making a rapid fortune, and seemed likely to gain his object, judging from the multitudes of working-men who poured into his till the fruits of their daily toil, earned by the sweat of their brow. And, of poor, pale, haggard women, and even young boys and timid girls, not a few added to his gains.

There was a "bar," and, within, a "bar-parlor;" and there on the last Saturday of a closing year sat a respectable-looking man with a book of entry and a money-bag before him. He was paying workmen; and it did not seem to strike him to notice at all how few of those men, as they passed out with their money, got beyond the enticements of the tap. It was not his business,— that was to pay money, not to superintend the spending of it. Was he the keeper of other men's characters and consciences? What right had he to interfere with them out of the work-yard? Ah, just the right, springing from our common relationship, to speak a kind "word in season" when temptation abounds, and resistance is rather doubtful. The foreman, however, would have found it difficult to warn the men against the temptations of the "bar" while paying their wages in the "bar-parlor."

The last man was paid, and, passing through the bar, was quitting the uncongenial scene, when he was accosted by the landlord, who, with his hands in his pockets, was complacently observing the constant succession of comers, and waiting until the last moment to count up the contents of the till. "Why, how's this?" said he; "surely you are not going without drinking your master's health, and doing something for the good of the house?"

———

"I never drink for compliment, sir," replied the man.

"What, not even to-night, to wish the old year well out and the new one in? Come, it will do you good; and it shan't be said that I'm none the better by a pint or so for one of D——'s men."

"I'm very much obliged to you," replied the workman, steadily; "but I can wish you well without drink. I wish you a happy new year with all my heart. May the Lord bless you, and show you the right way to be happy."

"What, then perhaps you don't think I'm just in it, Mr. Parson, eh?"

The name of the Lord was not "as ointment poured forth" in his hearing, evidently.

"I don't judge anybody, sir; I only expressed what I wish for everybody. If they know the right way, they won't be offended, I'm sure; and if they don't, my wish could not be better timed."

Some of the noisy crowd, who had been shouting, laughing, and swearing, caught the conversation and paused to listen.

"You don't mean to say there's any harm, I hope, in a jug of my good ale, or a glass of spirits and water, after a week's hard work; so, why can't you do as others do? Out with your argument if you've got one. I'm not afraid of a regiment of total-abstinence fellows, I promise you."

"Sir, excuse me," replied the honest speaker, in a low voice; "but, if you would walk with me to the street where I am living, I could show you twelve or fourteen arguments against stopping here to drink after wages are paid. There are poor women waiting for money to buy to-morrow's dinner; there are children whose shoes can't be got for school and church till the father takes home money to pay for the making or mending. Drinking men can't get credit even for a day, if it's known; and the very soap that's to wash the shirts on their backs has to be got yet, before their wives' day's work is done. I know what I'm saying, sir, I assure you. Good-night, sir."

" Stuff, nonsense, all a got-up tale," cried the landlord, as he angrily turned away; for the speaker was quickly beyond the flare of the " Red Lion;" and, while the uproarious group were laughing and shouting, " A saint! a saint!" the landlord went in to share brandy and water at the master's expense with the foreman of the D—— works.

The Christian workman hurried along; and, as he turned into the street where he dwelt, a woman with a basket on her arm came past. Poor thing! she too had been to the " Red Lion," and begged a few shillings from her husband, who was sitting in the bar; and with them she was hastening to get provisions and necessaries for the family, which could not be got in the immediate neighborhood; the rest she would run out for the next morning. And now, instead of sitting down to calm and soothe her spirit, and retire to rest in peace, her day's work seemed beginning in earnest. She had so much to do, that it was impossible to tidy up at all before she slept. - True there was no supper to get that night, for her husband never wanted any after finishing the week at the " Red Lion ; " and a crust and a drink of water would do for her while she worked. Then he never got up until very late on Sunday morning, and was so cross that the longer he lay in bed the better. So poor Mrs. Barnes settled it, at last, that if the drink on Saturday night made him idle, and kept her up till after midnight, it made him sleep on Sunday long enough to save his temper from troubling his family for an extra two or three hours.

The fact is, Barnes was a weak man, with light enough in his mind to know what was right, and without grace in his heart to cause him to do it; therefore his conscience was quite uneasy until he succeeded in drowning its voice. Alas! that may soon be done when we turn from its warnings, and set ourselves to do evil. He had been led astray first by that very plea which had just been tried on his fellow-workman, — the propriety of "doing as others did;" and when conscience in a sober hour reproved him, he was cross with all around him.

Barnes · had married a thoughtless young servant-girl, who, after a brief period of comparative comfort, was now the hard-working mother of five children, trying to keep them as decently as she could, but sadly deficient in method and management. She was full of grumbling discontent, and living without God in the world, because she thought she had not time to find him, and supposing that her hardships in this world would be set against any want of personal religion that otherwise might affect her acceptance in the next. Religion, she thought, was intended for the rich; certainly not for poor women with large families, and not very temperate husbands.

Long ere Mrs. Barnes and many like her had left the wash-tub, or seen the embers die out in the little grate before which the Sunday pinafore, or shirt, or gown, was drying for the next day's wear, the chimes of the old parish church had rung the dirge of the passing year, and welcomed in with a vigorous clang the moment of a new year's birth. But what mattered it that time was flying fast, which brought so little change to them? They best knew the proof in the wear and tear of health and strength, and the increase of trouble and anxiety. The pleasant chimes sang no news that affected them, unless, indeed, an over-powering sensation of the weariness and sameness, year after year, of a toiling, striving life, brought a flood of tears to the heart's relief.

But need it be so? Oh, no. There is for the poor man's wife as loving a smile to cheer, as strong an arm to sustain, and as rich a hand to bless, as for the truest Christian lady in the land, who brings her cares and burdens to a dear Saviour's feet. The difference is not in rank, position, wealth, or education; it is between that state of heart which is content to go grumbling through life without God and his grace, and that which looks up from the appointments of his providence in sweet assurance of the love that dictates all, and affectionate obedience to the word which connects all real happiness with faith in Jesus Christ.

There was one lovely contrast, however, in that very street. The Christian workman passed on to his home, — which, though very inferior to any they had known before, was like home to him now; for his wife and three children were there. The one room to cook and wash and eat and sit in was neat and clean; the fire was laid ready for lighting in the morning; and the breakfast things stood ready on a side-table, with a clean cloth thrown over them. The husband's shoes (though there is no denying that it is very proper for a working-man to clean his own dirty shoes) were as bright as those of any gentleman in the town; for it was a very loving, indulgent wife who presided over this humble home; and she never thought it a trouble to do anything to please her husband, and make him look as well as feel respectable and cared for. So the shoes stood ready, and two little pairs beside them, looking as tidy and trim almost as new.

And though by understood arrangement, the fire was not burning after ten o'clock, hearts were warm with love and thankfulness; and William and Susan sat and talked, and read the word of life together; and, while the sweet bells played in the new-year's morn, they knelt in earnest self-dedication before the God of all their mercies, as the first act on the record of another span of time, and the best offering in their power to Him to whom they owed their all.

> "The past they own with grateful praise:
> The future, be it years or days,
>   They fearless leave to Him,
> Whose loving kindness full and free,
> In Jesus' life and death, they see
>   Has put away their sin.
>
> "If they are Christ's, with him 'joint heirs,'
> 'All things' in heaven and earth are theirs,—
>   All fears are soothed to rest;
> While in his marred and loving face
> God's blended attributes they trace,
>   And know His will is best."

The new year came in with the day of rest. The first day of the week was new-year's day; and very pleasant it was to associate with the first hours of a new period of time the hallowed peace and refreshing services of the " Lord's day."

For the first time, too, the little child, watched with delight by its patrons, Robert and Milly, lay in its mother's arms during morning service, and behaved with surprising propriety ; so that it seemed no impossible thing for a whole family to be present together under certain good management, and with certain willing hearts. Susan could have gone out if her child had been restless ; but she was not one of those mothers who seem to think the possession of a baby is a perpetual excuse for neglecting many things that ought to be done, and doing many wilful things that had better be left undone.

The good pastor, whose sermon claimed their solemn and interested attention, gave a new-year's motto to the Christians present, — " My grace is sufficient for thee," — and supposed many cases for its valuable application. " And so it is, Susan," said William, as they walked home together. And the sight of Mrs. Barnes at work sweeping, and looking fagged and miserable as they passed her house, reminded him of its encouraging assurance for a trying duty which he thought he saw before him.

II.

A Fellow-Helper.

T'S little enough for a week's hard work, — isn't it?" remarked a tall, stout fellow-workman to William Taylor, jingling his money with his hand in his pocket, as they walked away from the Red Lion together after receiving their wages one Saturday night.

"It's honestly earned, at any rate," replied William.

"And you mean it to be honestly spent, — don't you, now, — mine as well as your own?" said the other, with a significant smile. "I caught your eye as I passed the tap."

"I felt a bit anxious, I confess," said William. "It would be worse than the sow returning to her wallowing in the mire, if you go back to your drink after keeping sober and manly for these few weeks past. Do you know, when I got you home that time, and saw your fine, strong frame, and the noble head of a man that was first made in the image of God, lie in the helplessness of childhood and the silliness of an idiot, through your own sin and folly, I felt hot tears of shame come into my eyes. Is this a man?— I thought to myself,— and more still, a husband and a father?"

"And you resolved to save me if you could, and bring back strength to the arm and sense to the head of the idiot. And yet I struck you, Taylor,—

fool that I was. You can't say I was helpless then."

" No, you had become a madman then. Drunkards go through all the characters that the devil has invented to dishonor man; until, at last, having disgraced themselves and done as much mischief as they can here, he has them to torment forever, unless they repent and seek forgiveness through Christ."

" I wonder you forgave me, Taylor. I couldn't forgive a blow."

" Did you ever say, ' Forgive us our trespasses, as we forgive them that trespass against us?' " asked Taylor. " There's a deal of meaning in those words." And the two men walked on in silence.

" I was saying our wages are little

enough for families like ours," at last remarked Freeman.

"Well, the times aren't the most prosperous for everybody just now, you know; and employers can't alter all their ways to suit them as easy as you and I can. They have to pay many a tax that never touches us; they have many a loss that we know nothing about; and yet, if their credit is to stand, business must go on, on, on. I've seen the anxious look and pale cheek of more than one or two among masters, while the men took their own as usual, never heeding the thoughts that made the hand tremble that paid them."

"I never thought of that, to be sure," said Freeman. "You've got a queer way of turning one's notions upside down."

"Don't you remember the Lord's apostles were accused of turning the world upside down, when they only wanted to set things in their right places?" answered William. "To my mind there's too much difference and too great distance between masters and workmen; but the fault is as much on our side as theirs, depend upon it."

"Why, they are rich, and we are poor; they want their work done, and we do it for them. Sure that's a mighty difference, and no fault of ours that I can see."

"Well I never could look upon my employer as nothing better than a cash-box," returned Taylor; "and I see no harm in lessening the distance between him and me, by thinking of him as the same flesh and blood, the servant of the same great Master, and, if he follows the Lord Jesus Christ, the sharer of the same blessed home in the world to come."

" Ah, you should say that to employers: it would do them more good than saying it to us poor fellows that they like to tread upon in this world."

" I've never seen the master yet that dared to tread upon an honest workman, who was doing his duty before God and man," said Taylor, warmly; " but I have seen many a workman trying or wishing to drag down them that God has set above him, like a madman pulling his own roof about his head. No, no; this is just the distance I mean: there's too much expected from employers, and too little felt for them by their dependents. Men have come to think of each other only in the place where they see one another, and forget that each has his duties and temptations, and afflictions and trials, and should feel for each other in twenty ways that have nothing to do with the work-shop or the pay-office."

"Well," returned Freeman, "I don't believe our master thinks we're made of anything but a couple of hands to do his work, and as many feet to carry us to it."

"I'm sorry to hear that, for I'm thinking of trying what he does think of us; and, if a few steady men will stand by me, I expect we can show him what stuff we are made of."

"You, Will. Taylor? Why, you don't

mean to strike,—do you? I thought you said you were contented with your wages?" exclaimed Freeman, in eager surprise.

"There, isn't it as I said?—you think of a master in his cash-box, and want as much out of it as you can get. I am thinking of him in his place before God, who will call him to account for other responsibilities than his money. No, I'm not going to strike; but I am going to try, God helping me, to speak a few words of truth, humbly and quietly, and see if something better than wages can't be got by it."

"I'll stand by you, be it what it may," said Freeman.

"Well, then, don't you think, if your good wife had her share of your wages in good time on Saturday, she might have things comfortable, and get some of her family, and perhaps herself, to public worship on Sunday? And if we could be paid somewhere away from a public-house, don't you think some of us would be the better for being kept out of temptation? "

" The last I'm quite sure about," said Freeman; " but as to poor Martha, you see, we've a large family, and she's always at work somehow, and is in more fuss on a Sunday than any day in the week. How could the wages help that?"

" She's up the greater part of Saturday night, and she markets on Sunday morning: perhaps she's too anxious about your dinner. Now, if she could buy and prepare on Saturday afternoon, there need be no fuss on Sunday. If my wife had to stay at home and cook my dinner, instead of going to public worship, I should be ashamed to eat it."

" Ah, Taylor, good management is a great thing; and perhaps you've never been so very poor as to slip out of good ways without minding it."

" No; God forbid we ever should," said William, reverently; while his tall, sturdy companion remembered with shame the wretched reason why he and his had done so. He had poured down his throat the value of cloaks, hats, shoes, furniture, that should have made home and family neat and respectable; and now how dared he marvel that both were destitute and miserable?

"My wife is a good manager, I'm thankful to say," continued Taylor; "but many a poor man's wife might be the same, if she'd a little more of good thoughts in her head, and a deal less of dull care in her heart."

"You always argue everything into religion somehow, as if you could make one believe that religion has anything to do with good management," retorted Freeman, half testily.

"Just so," said Taylor, quietly.

"Well, I know my wife would laugh at your notions; but how do you make it out?"

"It's no mystery that I can see," answered William. "It's just believing and loving the Lord Jesus Christ, and knowing that he has taken us under his care, and will make everything work for our good, if we will but take up our cross and follow him. Now poverty is a cross, no doubt, and gives us the privilege of following him close; for he was so poor he 'had not where to lay his head;' but he always made the best of everything; and when he had but a few loaves to feed a field full of hungry people, he gave thanks and made it do."

"But that was a miracle, man. We can't do anything like that."

"Well, so it was; but I've often thought it's very like that when we take in thankfulness and faith what is provided for us, and make it go as far as it will: that is good management, I think, and I don't fear but the Lord will make it enough somehow. At any rate, the feeling that we are following his steps, and minding what he said, brings peace and contentment with little, that some who have much know nothing about. Better is a dinner of herbs where love to God is, than a stalled ox and hatred and indifference to him therewith."

" I never used to think it reverend and respectful to mix up religion with every thing in this sort of way," remarked Freeman, after a long pause.

" It's just the life and soul of everything," returned William, earnestly. " Is not Jesus Christ the foundation of everything good? Can there be anything pleasing to God that has not his own dear Son at the bottom of it? He's our rock; and the character and ways and doings and tempers that are built on him can't be shaken down or broken up by winds and waves of trouble."

" If it's as you say, I'm sure I wish poor Martha could go and learn all about it; but she thinks she can't ever get out of a Sunday."

" Well, if she really can't, — and she has indeed a deal to do, poor thing, — there's another way that she might begin with," said Taylor, thoughtfully.

" Ah, you mean she should read the Bible; and so she might, sure enough."

" No I don't. Paul said, speaking to wives who wanted to know something particular about the doctrine, ' Let them ask their own husbands at home.' "

" But if the husband knows nothing himself ? " asked Freeman, quickly.

"More's the pity, and shame too, in this Christian land. If a man has a wife and family, it's his bounden duty to help them all to know and do God's holy will. It's a teaching he'll never repent; and may be they'll bless him for it through life."

"Well, it's clear it isn't quite the thing to be running after one's provisions on a Sunday morning; and if we can help it any way I think we'd better," said Freeman, after another thoughtful pause.

"My heart sinks at the sight of these back streets on the Lord's day, Freeman: women and children in and out of the shops, that look just like any other day. Now, if there were no buyers, there would soon be no sellers."

"Ah, but you and I can't reform the streets like that, if we never went into a shop, nor bought a penn'orth of anything."

"No, but we should not be 'partakers of other men's sins;' we should clear our consciences in the sight of God, so far as wilful neglect of his law goes; and when a man reforms his own ways, there's no knowing where his good example may end."

"And do you mean to ask our masters to do anything towards it by paying wages in good time?"

"Yes; and if three or four steady men will stand by me, we'll ask the favor in the name of the Lord we want to serve and honor."

"Then perhaps it wont be of any

use for me to offer to go along with you," said Freeman, in a saddened tone.

"Yes it will," eagerly answered William. "You are steady now, and you mean, God helping you, to keep on so."

"Well, thank you for that; for I was afraid you'd be ashamed of your company before them that know what's past."

"I have sought your soul, and have pitied them that belong to you, Freeman, else I should never have sought your company; and, now that the Lord seems answering my prayer, I'm not likely to change my mind towards you."

"I'm thinking, Taylor, you might just drop in some evening, and talk a bit about things, and just ask for a Bible, — will you? and I'll take care to rummage one up ready for you. And then perhaps you wouldn't mind saying a bit of a prayer for us, and may be things might get different by degrees, you see."

"That I will, the Lord permitting, and with all my heart," replied William.

"And, Taylor," added Freeman, with some hesitation, "you needn't be saying that text before Martha yet, you know, about asking husbands at home. If she takes to the Bible, she'll find it out sharp enough for herself; and I'd like to be ready if she did try it; for I'll warrant she'd wonder enough how I learned any good."

"The Lord God the Holy Spirit will teach you if you ask him," said Taylor, solemnly; and the rough hands of the fellow-workmen joined in a hearty grasp.

They were most likely friends for life, and the working-man in the working-man's home was the best Scripture reader or home missionary that could enter there.

Martha, who would have been in a great fuss at the approach of a formal visitor in clerical costume, was no wise daunted at the sight of her husband's friend, who had been the means of keeping him sober for several weeks; and, when he led the conversation heavenward, she paused to listen, drew near, and hushed two or three troublesome children who were interrupting, heard a few words of Scripture read out of a book that mysteriously appeared from somewhere, and was surprised into kneeling down and an attempt to pray.

A wholesome train of thought arose

within her; she looked back on her past life, and burst into tears; and by and by she will look forward with hope, and upward with smiles, and will know that God is the working-man's friend, and the gracious helper of the working-man's wife in all her trials, and will encamp around their humble dwelling with a love as true, and a care as great, as ever were manifested in days of miracles; with this only difference, that those who walk with him by faith are privileged to glorify him more than those who walked by sight.

III.

Grievances and Remedies.

"IN all thy ways acknowledge God, and he shall direct thy paths." So read William Taylor ere quitting his home for work.

"You wont forget me to-day, Susan," he said as the children scrambled up into his arms for the parting kiss. "I'm not much given to meddle with matters that may be thought too high for such as I, but many will be benefited if I succeed, and none harmed if I fail."

Susan did not forget; and her humble home duties were not the worse performed, because now and then, from the depth of her affectionate heart, rose up, in the midst of them, a prayer for her brave husband in the warfare of life.

There is "a time to speak" as well as "a time to keep silence;" and the word which no mere personal inconvenience would have urged from the quiet Christian workman must be spoken for the honor of God and the good of immortal souls.

At twelve o'clock the foreman was requested to inform Mr. D—— that a few of his men asked leave to speak to him at any time he would be pleased to appoint.

"What is it about?" said Mr. D——, hastily. "Are they dissatisfied with anything? Because those who don't like my service are at liberty to leave it."

"They have some request to make, I believe, sir; but they wish to see you themselves about it."

"Quite useless, you can tell them; for I am not one to yield to the evil spirit of the times, which is for changing the places of masters and workmen."

Seeing, however, a cluster of heads near his office, Mr. D—— stuck his pen in his hair, put on his hat with a resolute, made-up-mind sort of look, and putting his hand in his pockets came and stood at the door to contemplate his petitioners. Among them were two known until recently, according to the foreman's estimate, as good workmen, but sad drunken fellows.

William Taylor stepped forward, and, in a few simple, respectful words, stated the wish of the majority of the men to be paid somewhere away from the temptations of a public-house, and at an hour more convenient for the comfort of their homes and the observance of the Lord's day.

Mr. D—— was not prepared for requests like these. He expected something about increase of wages, or shorter hours, and was for the moment as much at fault as if he had heard for the first time that his men had homes, and were as much bound as himself to respect the fourth commandment.

" I should not have supposed, from the recommendation your former employers took the trouble to write for you, that a public-house was a temptation to you," at last he said, looking with a half-doubting, sarcastic expression at Taylor.

" Sir, he speaks for me," — " and for me," eagerly interrupted the two reformed men; " there's no fear for him; but he has seen what it is to others."

" As to what you say about the inconveniences of evening payment, it only proves the bad management of the week that you are penniless on a Saturday. I do not consider it my business at all."

" Sir," replied Taylor, " we do not deny that in some cases there may be bad management; but only those who live from hand to mouth, as it were, know the difficulties of managing well with families to provide for; and with means to do better, if the opportunity is given,

the blame of Sunday trading and god-
less homes will fall in the right place. I
would respectfully say that it would be
well to take away all excuse; for if
some of us can slide our sins upon other
people's shoulders, justly or unjustly, we
aren't likely to mend."

"Well, if anything should incline me
to your way of thinking, you will hear
of it. At present I don't think of
making any changes."

No one seeing Mr. D—— as he turned
abruptly away from his men, at that
moment under a thorough misconception
of the nature of their relative positions,
would have thought him the same who,
an hour afterwards, trod with noiseless
step and anxious tenderness the sick
chamber of his children.

"I'm afraid we have not chosen a good time, friends," said William Taylor to his companions; "there's something wrong, but we can't help it. Let us wait patiently and leave our cause in higher hands."

On the following morning Mr. D—— was accompanied by a fine, bright boy, who ran about the premises peeping at the workmen and seeming very much disposed to be friendly with some of them; but he was watched and called off perpetually by his father, who dreaded such contact for the child.

At last, dragging his father by the hand towards the place where William Taylor was at work, he begged hard to be allowed to see the working of the machinery.

"My dear boy, it is dangerous: you must not go there."

"Oh, papa, this man will take care of me, wont you now?" he cried, looking pleadingly at William.

"Is there no risk? Can you spare a minute for him?" said Mr. D——, following up his boy's request.

"If you think proper, sir; and I'll take the care of him that I would of my own," replied William, respectfully.

"Well then, Archy, keep close; mind what is said to you; and, when you wish, you can come back to me;" and, instinctively certain that the boy would be safe, Mr. D—— left him with his new friend.

Archy was not to be shaken off after his first curiosity had been gratified;

and he chatted away, revealing several little circumstances connected with his family, which William heartily wished he had known before.

" I shall ask to come again to-morrow," said the child, as he was called to return home; " and mamma will let me if my sisters are no better. The doctors will come again to-night to see them."

The next morning Archy bounded across the yard to claim acquaintance.

" How are your little sisters ? " asked William.

" Very ill, — no better," answered Archy, becoming serious in a moment. " Mamma was crying when she kissed me at coming away with papa. Oh, here's papa, and I want to stay with you, — may I ? Papa, may I stay with this kind man ?

I like him very much; he can tell me many nice things; he has got a little boy just as old as I am."

"If you promise not to hinder, you can stay a little while."

"Sir," said William, raising his cap as Mr. D—— stood before him, "I feel very sorry that we intruded our little troubles upon you just when you are called to bear great ones. Your son has told me what shows it was not a right time."

"Oh, it is of no consequence," hastily said Mr. D——, surprised at the delicacy and sympathy of a common workman; but no, alas! not a common one either, though many with hearts as kind lack courage for the straightforward, opportune expression of their feeling.

" Yes, sir, it is of consequence, foi you must have enough to think about just now; and I only wish we had known it somehow."

" Why," said Mr. D——, " you would not have me bring my domestic anxieties into the work-yard, — would you ? "

" Yes, sir, that's just what I would," replied William. " We can all see that something is going wrong, and we've hearts as well as hands, and know how to feel for them that are above us as well as for each other."

" I should have thought you would wonder what you had to do with my private feelings."

" It's a mistake, sir; we are all the same flesh and blood; and if we do your work with a good will, we should regard all your concerns with kindly interest. One word to show that you cared for our sympathy would have brought all hearts here round you in no time; and though we can't help you ourselves, may be the prayer to Him who can would not be despised."

" You have children," said Mr. D——, in an altered voice.

"I have, sir; and I pray God to spare you the pain of parting from yours."

Mr. D—— held out his hand,—a rush of new feelings bursting through the icy barriers of pride and caste; and the rough palm of the working-man grasped it with honest pleasure. It was the "one touch of nature that makes the whole world kin;" the electric message of a humanity common to each,

and the pledge of a relationship honor
able to both.

.   .   .   .

" You needn't fear, sir," said the foreman, as he saw an anxious glance
searching across the yard for Archy;
" the young gentleman is safe enough
with Taylor. The yard isn't like the
same since Taylor joined us; for those
who don't care to listen to his good
words begin to take heed he shan't
hear so many of their bad ones."

" Do you believe his wife ever markets on a Sunday ? " asked Mr. D——,
glad of an opportunity to hear something more.

" No, sir; she's quite a different sort
of person from that. He is speaking
for others, not for himself. I once had

a bit of a grudge against people who pretended to be more religious than their neighbors; but, sir, to my mind, this man's religion has got something real and practical about it."

" Well, then, since you see the difference, you can keep your grudge against pretenders if you like; but let us honor the real thing wherever we are favored to find it."

The foreman was pleased; for, though there was not much in the words, they were spoken in a tone of unusual urbanity and kindness. After all, Mr. D—— was not above profiting by a lesson when he was happy enough to receive one.

For some days little Archy was a constant visitor, and then he came no more. Sickness had prostrated him also; and very sad was the look with which Mr. D—— responded to William's daily inquiry for the child. It was a fiery ordeal for the parents as they saw each little life threatened with dismissal; but after long and severe suffering, they all rallied through it, and the worst features of their complaint then seized upon Mr. D—— himself, worn as he was with long nights of watching in almost hopeless anxiety. But he also recovered, and with his whole family was ordered off to spend the winter in a milder climate.

William Taylor had been a daily inquirer at the house, frequently apologizing for giving the trouble of answering him, but always receiving a kind assurance from the servants that they were glad to see him; for he was often mentioned by Master Archy in his illness. So it was not wonderful that, when the carriage was at the door to convey the family away, the coachman's assistance was gently set aside, and the kind hands of William Taylor lifted his little friend into it.

"I'm getting well,— I'm coming to see you again," whispered the pale child, smiling in William's face; "you'll show me the engine again,— wont you?"

Then came Mr. D—— himself, so reduced, so altered, that William could scarcely conceal his feeling at the sight; and the master rested his hand on the workman's strong arm to help him to his seat, and then drove away in search of health and strength.

In the mean time alterations had been making progress at the small office in the work-yard; and on Saturday afternoon a notice appeared outside the door, — " Wages paid here; dismiss at four o'clock."

The foreman stood there to observe the effect upon the men, who chiefly read and passed on with a triumphant smile. But there was only humble thankfulness on Taylor's countenance. He knew the value of the boon, and rejoiced in the triumph of principle over covetousness and indifference. It was a proof, too, that a working-man's cause may command attention when stated with straightforward earnestness and common sense; while threats and violence only provoke opposition, and widen the estrangement of those who should support, encourage, and help one another.

"Three cheers for William Taylor!" shouted one of the men. "He has done us a good turn, and we shan't forget it."

"And as for the Red Lion, I don't know but what I shall go in once more just to drink his health," said another slyly.

"Take care you don't injure your own by it, Barnes," said William, nodding to him as he passed on.

"He's a right brave chap, that," said Barnes. "I wish I'd got half his notions."

"You can get them where he got them, if you've a mind, I dare say," said Freeman. "I'm looking after them myself."

"Why, where?"

"Just out of his Bible, and nowhere else. It's an honest old book, that never flatters one, you know. Bad is bad and no mistake; and good is good of the right sort. We'll all find our pictures there if we look for them."

Three months passed away, and then Mr. D—— reappeared among his men with a step as firm and a mien as erect as ever. They had learned when to expect him, and, as soon as he entered the yard, they gathered round to greet him with a hearty British welcome, thanking him for conceding their wishes, and assuring him that if work needed finishing after the hour appointed for dismissal, they would willingly stay and do it, rather than allow him to be a loser by his kindness.

Mr. D—— turned to thank them, but his heart was full; he was surprised, and for the moment overpowered, and, instead of the word he would have spoken, he held out his hand, which every man in the group pressed forward to grasp with genuine pleasure, and then turned off to his work with a feeling that would, if need be, risk life and limb to serve him.

IV.

Struggle and Victory.

THERE are two classes of character among working-people; one,
the prudent, who strive to keep
out of difficulties; and the other,
by far the more numerous of the two,
who sink under them, with a miserable
idea that they were "born to bad luck,"
and, once down, it is labor in vain to try
to rise above them again. Left to their
idle fatalism, they fall lower and lower,
until their sad history often ends in
workhouses, jails, and penal servitude.
Happy are those to whom some whisper comes that bad may be made better

instead of worse, and to whom a hand is stretched out to help as an earnest of its truth! So God deals with fallen sinners, and so should his redeemed deal with their fallen neighbors.

It is very pleasant to witness thrift and industry, and to commend them accordingly. But it is perhaps more pleasant still to behold the upward struggle; the tear of penitence that gladdens angels; the successful effort that shakes off the stupor of despair. In this hopeful stage was poor Martha Freeman's experience, as she tapped one Saturday afternoon at Mrs. Taylor's door.

"May I come in a minute?" said she. "I'm so glad you are at home, and Mr. Taylor not here just now."

"Oh, yes, pray come in," said Susan,

cheerfully, and setting a chair for her visitor, who looked very worn and tired. "You wont mind me going on with my work, I'm sure." Susan was running a string into a clean curtain for the clean window.

"Please don't let me hinder you. But, dear, dear, what a nice smell of something cooking!"

"It isn't very nice at this time of day, I think," said Susan, smiling; "but it's our dinner getting ready for to-morrow."

"It's all quite true what Freeman says," ejaculated Martha, looking round with a sigh; "our room is never a bit like yours. I used to say no place could be decent with a drunken husband; but Freeman is sober now, and we don't seem much better yet."

"Oh, but you will be by and by. Don't be cast down, Mrs. Freeman; step by step, you know, brings us up the hill at last."

"I've made up my mind to go marketing no more on Sunday," said Martha; "but I've not been used to get things ready the day before, like you; and now that I've got the money in good time, I came to ask you, Mrs. Taylor, how I'd best do. Might I know what's cooking there for your dinner to-morrow?"

"To be sure," said Susan; "just come and look;" and she lifted the lid of the steaming pan; "it's a beef stew, which is both very good and economical, and makes us a good many dinners, if done carefully. See, here are the bones, — they

Willie occupying his father's chair.   Chap. 9.

stewed all yesterday afternoon ; " and she took a plate of perfectly whitened bones from the cupboard.

" Dear me, did they come as clean as that ? "

" Not quite ; but this is what I got off them at the last, and with a little of the liquor put to the bits nicely seasoned, and a small bit of bacon chopped among them, it is something for my husband's supper or breakfast, you see ; " and Martha looked admiringly upon a gelatinous mass formed in the bottom of a basin, which Susan turned over upon a plate and begged her to taste.

" It's beautiful," said Martha ; " it's just like a dish that used to go on the breakfast-table where I lived housemaid. Why, Mrs. Taylor, your husband must

5

live like a gentleman if you do things for him like this."

"Why should he not?" said Susan, smiling. "He wants his meals just as much; and if a little handiwork and a little painstaking will make things look nice as well as wholesome with no extra expense, why shouldn't it be done for one's husband as well as for one's master? William doesn't encourage any extravagance, I assure you; but he knows I like to make everything as nice as I can for him out of what we can afford to buy."

"Ah, I dare say you lived cook somewhere and learned how."

"No, I was a nursemaid when I was in service; but I learned a little of anything useful whenever I could, and it's

come in very well for me since. The
thing is, I think, in keeping one's home
comfortable, to do everything in the very
best way we can, and never let untidy,
make-shift ways get the upper hand; for
they're much harder to shake off than
nice clean ways are to begin with."

Mrs. Freeman knew this very well;
but she said, "It's very hard to do
things nice though when you're in a
hurry."

" There's a text that keeps me up to
it," said Susan, modestly, " if I may just
say it to you, Mrs. Freeman. I'm sure
you'll think it ought, since our Lord provided it for just such as you and me,
knowing our difficulties and temptations:
' Whatsoever ye do in word or deed, do
all in the name of the Lord Jesus,

giving thanks to God and the Father by him.' You know we couldn't be untidy and slovenly in the name of the Lord,—could we? nor 'give thanks' to him for things that we didn't strive to use the very best way in our power."

"Well, I'm sure it seems there's nothing like the Bible for keeping people right. Perhaps, if I'd minded it before, I shouldn't have been as I am now; but the truth is, Mrs. Taylor, Freeman has set his heart upon me going to church with him to-morrow morning; and though I said I'd rather wait till we get better off, and things comfortable about us again, he said it was no use waiting; we must begin to make things better at once, and at the right end too, which, he says is to go and hear the Lord's message in his own gospel, on his own day, and show him we want to be under his blessing; and I can't put him off, though I told him I wasn't fit to go as a respectable woman ought to go."

"Oh, don't try to put him off," said Susan, entreatingly; "go any way; never mind the outside; 'for the Lord looketh upon the heart,' you know."

"And that's a deal shabbier than my gown, if I dared but look into it. So you see I can't stop at home to cook anything for dinner, and I want to have a bit of meat done nice; for we've only had potatoes these two days past, because we want our money to get things out of the pawn as soon as ever we can."

"There's no time for a stew like this

now," said Susan, thoughtfully, " for the real good of it consists in its being properly done." Then, after a minute, she added, " I dare say you've got something to do yet; so if you just get a bit of meat as you go home, and if you wont think it officious of me, Mrs. Freeman, I shall be very glad to come and help you for half an hour by and by; and when you've washed the children and got them to bed, we can soon think of something for their dinner to-morrow when all the rest is done."

Washed the children! Mrs. Freeman had no regular time for washing children, and she looked somewhat confounded at this new item in the list of duties. That it would be well to consider it, however, she was very sure, for not an hour ago she had denounced two or three of them as "the dirtiest grubs that ever lived."

"I'm sure I'll be very much obliged to you," said the poor woman, gratefully; "for I just feel as if I should give up trying to do right because everything is wrong; and we are so down in the world now, it seems as if it wasn't worth while to struggle against it;" and the tears sprang to her eyes.

"Oh, yes, indeed it is, for your husband's sake, who is likely to be kinder and better to you than ever he was, — for your dear children's sake, who are old enough to profit by your example, — for your own sake, dear Mrs. Freeman, for God loves you, and has put it into your heart to wish to do right. Don't trouble about to-morrow, but let it be a happy day for you all."

"You are very kind," said Martha. "I will try, — yes, I will; and you'll show me your way to make up something when you come." And away she went with a lighter heart. Somebody would put a hand to her burden to save her from being crushed under it. Oh, precious sympathy! the kindness of a queen with wealth at her disposal could not have done for Martha the true effectual benefit which Susan conferred when she offered her sisterly hand to share the actual drudgery of redeeming her neglected home.

A bright thought had struck Susan; and when William came home, and she told him what had occurred, he willingly agreed to it. So, after the little one was in bed, leaving Robert and Milly to entertain their father, she set off, after her own not very light day's work, to assist her poor neighbor in preparing for a new manner of Sunday life.

She carried with her a large covered jar, and, peeping in at the door to see that nobody was in the way, she found Mrs. Freeman washing one of the children by the fireside; and much the little creature seemed to enjoy its bath.

" All the others are done," said Mrs. Freeman, " except Maggy and Johnny, who are gone with father to get each a pair of shoes, instead of my best gown out of pawn. I couldn't let the poor things go barefoot on Sunday any more, and now they can go to church."

"That will be very nice; but you don't give up going yourself, Mrs. Freeman, I hope?" said Susan, anxiously.

"No; but I minded what you said about the Lord looking on the heart, and I said to myself, 'Why should I mind about my gown if I couldn't have a better one just yet? So down with your foolish pride, Martha Freeman;' and it's almost gone. My old cotton gown will be clean; I've taken care of that. See, it's all ready for ironing there."

"And I've brought you my large merino mantle, Mrs. Freeman, if you'll please to wear it till you get your own things again; it can't serve a better purpose. Don't speak of it; you're very, very welcome. I'm sure there are good times in store for you yet. Now may I put in an iron and do the gown while you get the water away, and the hearth swept up?"

"Thank you; but the dinner, you know; I would rather you would tell me about that. I got a few bits of meat as I came along, but they are only a shabby dinner, after all, except I can cook them your way."

"Well, William and I want you to do us the kindness to accept half of our stew for to-morrow, Mrs. Freeman; and I think it will serve you all if you do a few potatoes to eat with it."

The poor woman was overwhelmed with amazement. Why, how could they afford such a present? Not often, certainly; but both the generous donors would rather have gone without any dinner at all than suffer Freeman's wish to be disappointed on the morrow, or his poor, anxious wife to be overcome by her many difficulties just when she was trying to meet them in a right spirit. What a burden was removed! All the family would be fed comfortably; and before Sunday came round again, Martha would be better prepared with provision for it. Herrings and bits of bacon, however good in their way, would no longer be the Sunday resource for Saturday's poverty or mismanagement, and the neighboring shops would miss one customer from the graceless throng who jostled one another at the counter or stall, in haste, covetousness, or dishonesty.

Susan, having ironed the gown, and done sundry little kindnesses besides, and seeing the room neater and nicer than it had been for many a week, had scarcely escaped from Mrs. Freeman's earnest thanks, when the father and his two children, in a perfect ecstasy over new shoes, came in. There was a little more washing to be done then, after which Martha was able to sit down and rest; and her husband, looking round with an approving smile, said it was a blessing to feel happier at " home " than ever he had felt at the Red Lion in all his life.

Sunday morning at half-past six o'clock found Martha stirring. It was a great effort, which only those who have conquered self-indulgence in the particu-

lar snare of dozing away the early hours
of the Sabbath morning can appreciate.
All honor to those who have been thus
victorious.   But Martha wanted things
comfortable before her husband got up;
and, moreover, she wanted the help of
her eldest girl in making them so.

"Maggy, dear Maggy, get up," she
whispered into a little closet that just
held the bed of three of the children.
"Come and help mother, Maggy, wont
you, this morning?"

"What is it, mother?" said the child,
rubbing her sleepy eyes.

"It's Sunday, dear, and we're going
to church to-day, you know; and I want
to be all in time."

"Oh, yes, and I've got new shoes.
I'll be down stairs in no time, mother."

Poor Maggy had very nearly fallen asleep again, notwithstanding the new shoes; but another gentle call, and she jumped up. The children were dressed, the fire lighted, and breakfast ready, when Freeman came downstairs. The sight of things there made him turn round and scramble back again quicker than he came; for how could he go and sit down with unwashed hands, un-combed hair, unshaven, and but half dressed, among those clean, smiling faces?

Martha had not forgotten to set him a basin of water, and the best towel she had, on the old drawers that served for a dressing-table; so there was no excuse, and as soon as he could he appeared again in another fashion before his assembled family. Now he could look as cheerful as any of them; he could hold the newly bought Bible and read a few verses of the gospel, and clasp a pair of clean hands in a short, earnest prayer for clean hearts and right spirits to be bestowed on himself and the kneeling group around him.

And brave, victorious Martha went to church in her old cotton gown, covered nicely though it was with Susan's mantle, and a shabby old bonnet which had neither cap within nor ribbons without, but a pair of washed strings to hold it on, which she wisely thought better than dirty streamers; but there was a clean, bright face inside it, and a sense of peaceful self-respect, better than all the finery of a milliner's show-room.

May God's blessing meet thee, sister,
and all like thee, who, triumphant in His
strength, thus struggle upward and on-
ward over pride, vanity, idleness, and
the thousand hindrances that seem to
stand like "lions in the way."

6

V.

Sympathy and Help.

ELL, to be sure, what can she want here, I wonder?" exclaimed Mrs. Barnes, involuntarily putting her hands to her head to feel that her cap was there, and to tuck up her hair under it; then dashing some straggling things, unsightly to behold except in their right places, into an inner room, she went forward to admit the lady who stood at her door. There was no appearance of tracts to denote a district visitor. The lady was pleasant-looking and very plainly dressed; and much Mrs. Barnes wondered what brought her there, as she offered a chair, and, standing before her, waited to be addressed.

" Wont you sit down also ? " said the lady, who, lady though she was, seemed embarrassed and uncomfortable and nervous. " I have only called to become acquainted with you. Your husband works for mine, and so I thought we ought to feel a little interest in each other."

Mrs. Barnes was quite amazed. Then this must be Mrs. D——, and what in the world made her come now, — she that had never darkened the door of one of the work-people before ?

Ah, if Mrs. Barnes could have known what made her come now, she must have looked back a little while to the sick-house, where precious children and a beloved husband had lingered between life and death; where prayer had been offered in agony of heart, and answered in pitying love; where the affectionate interest of the Christian workman had been spoken of with surprise and plea- sure; and where the reception given to a restored master had not been without its influence on the heart of the gratified mistress.* How could she testify her gratitude to God and them better than by giving up a little of that personal ease and leisure to which the labor of their hands contributed, that she might min- ister to the well-being of their families, and at least acknowledge, as opportunity might permit, their claims on her sympa-

* See Tract Magazine, March, 1860, pp. 71 – 75

thy and notice ? This it was brought Mrs. D—— in the first warmth of her gratitude to search out, among back streets and courts and lanes, the dwellings of her husband's workmen. She was new and strange to the work; and, as only God could know the feelings which filled her heart, it was not surprising that the people on whom she called failed to respond encouragingly, and rather stared and wondered in vulgar silence than seemed disposed to adopt her as a friend on the spot.

Mrs. Barnes managed to mutter that she was much obliged, was very glad to see my lady, hoped the family were quite strong again; to all of which Mrs. D—— replied kindly, and then tried to lead her to speak of her own family, their

---

prospects, and occupations. Poverty evidently was here, and Mrs. D—— knew the cause; but she soon knew too that poor Mrs. Barnes was a grumbling slave, needing very much that some gentle voice should breathe sounds of peace and love over the inharmonious feelings that were hardening her heart against God and man. There was danger that if she succeeded in winning this poor woman's confidence, her tongue would burst all barriers, and an eloquent flood of complaints and wrongs would overwhelm the hearer, and crush any latent hope of rendering service in her unhappy circumstances.

But, just then, four or five children came rushing into the house, fresh primed from some scene of dirt and mischief, and quite disconcerted their mother, who would not for anything that their introduction to a new patroness should have occurred in this rude, uproarious style. In vain she commanded silence, threatened, scolded, and drove them out again; they were quite resolved to share the novelty of the lady's company, and pushed, scrambled, and quarrelled at the door until no other voice could be heard; and Mrs. D—— was glad to beat a retreat, promising to call again some time when Mrs. Barnes was "not so busy."

"Bless her, when does she suppose that is to be?" said Mrs. Barnes to herself. "Just like them though; they've got their leisure and forget that such as I have none. But she'll see how that is, come when she may."

Mrs. D—— had not found either Mrs. Freeman's improving family, or Mrs. Taylor's neat though humble dwelling; and, weary and dispirited, she paid a visit on the way home to the valued friend who had encouraged her to make the effort just commenced.

"I am afraid, dear Miss L——," said she, "I shall do no good after all. I don't know what to say to those I find living in wilful neglect of the common decency and comfort of home. It will never do to begin with finding fault."

"Certainly not," said Miss L——. "Have you found nothing to commend?"

"Very little indeed. I have seen dirty rooms, dirty children, slovenly women, until my heart aches to think what specimens of our sex are the mothers of the rising generation. The daughters will be a degree worse; and fathers, husbands, and brothers must seek elsewhere the companionship and comfort denied them at home. What can we do to help it?"

"Only be more earnest, prayerful, and persevering in what we are doing, I believe," said Miss L——. "We cannot go and clean their houses; but we may try to be more zealous in telling them of Him who cleanseth the heart, and trust that, in time, acquaintance with his purity and experience of his love may bear among its fruits the earthly proprieties of a Christian home."

"It requires very great determination and self-denial to stay long in some of their houses," said Mrs. D——.

"I know it does; but we can exercise that self-denial for Christ's sake, remembering what this world must have been to him as he moved about among its polluted population with the refinement and delicacy of his perfect senses and holy affections. Ours are but fallen senses, offended by fallen fellow-sinners and their ways. Think of the difference, my dear friend, while you try to tread in his steps. Indeed, I think you should draw, from what you have seen to-day, fresh incentives to exert your influence in correcting what you deplore."

"I believe you are right. I must not give up; but I wish I could feel less annoyance, and more pleasure in trying."

"May I say a word or two for, at least, some of our poor, dirty, slovenly sisters?" said Miss L——. "Doubtless, many of them set out in life with pleasant thoughts of how things were to be with them, and good intentions to do their duty well. Perhaps they were soon disappointed and undeceived, and found they had rested their earthly happiness on some broken reed. Knowing no higher nor better resting-place, they droop in spirit and grow discontented. Poverty threatens; a young family occupies time and fills the heart with care; and appliances to which they have been accustomed are sacrificed to fill hungry mouths, and keep a shelter overhead. Perhaps sickness depresses; and there is no energy left to rise out of the untidiness or the confusion in which they have become unintentionally involved. This frets the temper; temper spoils the countenance; and the once happy, light-hearted girl, who was bright as a May-day, shrinks and shrivels into crabbed, thriftless, premature age. Her children are a trouble; her worst characteristics overpower her better ones; she envies those who, she supposes, are better off, and considers her lot the hardest in creation. Poverty, sickness, and disappointment, unaccompanied by recognition of the will of God, and faith in his promises, are miserable enemies to domestic life, and are too often thought sufficient excuse for just what you have seen to-day. When I look on such a wreck, I try to trace back what she once was, and give her credit for at least having wished to do well. But think what it must be to lose all that made life seem pleasant, and to have nothing in prospect beyond it. There is no lever, as it were, to lift up the deadly weight that has fallen over the spirit; and a careless, hopeless manner of what they call 'putting on' from day to day serves their daily need."

"But, dear Miss L——, granting all this, surely they might use the little effort that would preserve cleanliness, if not order and industry."

"You forget that cleanliness requires energy, regularity, personal exertion; but the spring of all is gone."

"Then, doubtless, our best opportunity

is the moment when the heart feels the shadow of the first approaching sorrow, that we may try to forestall its influence, and point to the bow of promise on the passing cloud."

" And is it not worth ninety-nine disappointments if we meet with that opportunity in the hundredth attempt? I would not give up one case without being fairly driven from the field; but I admit that if we were in time to catch the first occasion, it might be a blessed moment .to the tried one. If the first hard thought were crushed, the first ill-humor subdued, the first reproach checked, the first rent repaired, the first child well trained, the first hours well employed, what different scenes might gladden the hearts and homes of all!"

"And may we not add, that the first day of the week well spent, the first thought of the morning given to God in praise and prayer, would so maintain the inner life that the external habits could not go very wrong?"

" Most assuredly. It is useless to attack the branches of the weed. We had better lay the axe to the root, and sow the good seed plentifully. Sin needs the sword of the Spirit to cut its way to the heart; and we need not look for a harvest if we have not sown the seed. Let us not be ' weary in well doing; for in due time we shall reap, if we faint not.' Let us bear with dirt and incivility and discomfort for one short hour, in hope to carry into the midst of them a

———

blessing that endureth forever. We may regret what we see, without affectation; but we cannot shrink from efforts to remedy it, without sin."

Mrs. D—— persevered, and another day brought before her the cheerful face and practical faith of Susan Taylor, who soon became a valuable assistant in the cause. Through her poor Martha Freeman's upward struggle gained help and sympathy, and Mrs. Barnes was encouraged with hope of brighter days. She said that her husband yielded to bad companions who induced him to drink, when, if he could have broken from them, his wishes were in favor of sobriety.

Mrs. D. found a remedy; and Barnes was favored with an opportunity to begin a fresh career in a new scene and among new associates. Mr. D—— had become the proprietor of a colliery in a neighboring county, and was sending men to assist in erecting new machinery. He had his own reasons for keeping William Taylor where he was; but, apparently without premeditation, asked him one day if he thought any hands on the premises might be trusted. As he expected, Freeman was immediately named, as being now a sober Christian man; and William then suggested that, if Barnes were transferred at the same time, it might be good for himself and his family.

"My wife and yours have settled that point already," said Mr. D——, smiling; "and now I want you to go over with them for a week or two only, just to see that they settle in decent cottages with all needful comfort about them, and not too near the public-house. I shall take care that they understand you go as a fellow-workman, while I shall feel that you go as my representative to fulfil a ·duty to my men. They both regard you as their best earthly friend, and will take advice from you which might seem intrusive from me. I heartily wish, Taylor, that these men's souls may help to brighten your heavenly crown."

Bright rose the glow of honest pleasure to the cheek of the Christian workman under this mark of his employer's confidence, while a little voice whispered softly at his heart, "Not unto me, O

Lord, not unto me be the praise; but
unto thee be the praise, for thy mercy
and thy truth's sake."

VI.

Cottage Cookery and Meals.

COOKING is not a very inviting subject, but it is one which very intimately concerns the real comfort of real life; and the useful more than the entertaining being the object of these pages, Mrs. Taylor's good management in that department of her duty, and the economical hints she could impart to her less practical neighbor, must not be omitted in this little record of her usefulness.

It was a pleasant time when the first wife of the human race, in the instinctive fulfilment of her natural duty, needed but to look round among the luxuriant productions of her beautiful neighborhood to find the banquet ready to her hand, wherewith to regale her husband after his healthful industry. But such elegant ease is not for her daughters She presumed upon indulgence, and made the fatal experiment which laid upon herself and them a burden of toil as well as sin; and the provision of daily food for the hungry husband and children is one of the household cares bequeathed to wives and mothers.

Whether this one was lessened or increased by the permission bestowed on Noah and his posterity that "every moving thing that liveth" might be meat for them, may not perhaps be worth inquiry; certain it is that animal food, especially in a climate like ours, is considered essential to the health and vigor of the human frame; and the eager question in humble life is not " How shall we cook it? " but rather " How shall we get it? "

When, however, in the kind providence of God, the meat is obtained, it is painful to see thankfulness marred, and temper irritated, by the ignorance or clumsiness with which the cook has contrived to spoil it. The good appetite acquired by honest industry without should be met by the good provision of the frugal manager within. To obtain the most nourishment out of the smallest quantity is the wisdom and duty of the working man's wife; and abundance of what is spoiled and unwholesome can

never compensate for the absence of genuine nutriment. Messes "warmed up"
three or four times over, meat burned
before the fire, or boiled at a furious
rate over it (as if fire, water, and cook
were all too late and must make it up
in sound and hurry), may look like a
meal, and fill a hungry stomach; but
they will not contribute to the vital
energy, nor help to maintain the purity
of that blood on which bodily health
depends. It would be well if there were
a little voice in every piece of meat to
say, " Now here I am; and it depends
on you, goodwife, whether I merely fill
a gap or diffuse my influence for good
through that manly frame, and minister
to the current of life which flows
through the heart that loves you dearly."

"You see, Mrs. Taylor," said Martha Freeman, as she anxiously inquired about "that beautiful Sunday dinner that was enjoyed so much," "meat is so expensive for us, while we want so many things before we get comfortable again."

"Yes, but little and good, you know, goes furthest after all; and, if I may take the liberty to say it, Mrs. Freeman, I think the bits of things people often buy to make up a short meal, that hasn't much real good in it after all, may cost more than a wholesome piece of meat to begin with. I don't hold with much salt meat any way; for cheap bacon is seldom good, and it's better to avoid things that make one thirsty if we can."

"Dear me!" cried Martha, "I never

thought of that; and very likely many a pint of ale has gone after the salt bacon and the red herrings that we've had to our potatoes."

"I always scald bacon, to take away some of the salt, before I fry it," said Susan; "and when eggs are cheap, we sometimes have them to it. But I think the cheapest dinners we have are made out of a shin of beef, that costs about one and ninepence or two shillings. Only the goodness comes with the stewing. I cut the meat off and stew the bones in water when I don't want the fire for anything else, taking care to keep the cover of the pan quite tight down, that it shouldn't waste away in steam; and it stews quietly for five or six hours, — that is, only the bones chopped through in several places. Then I pour the stew into an earthen pan to cool, and a cake of fat forms on the top that makes a bit of paste for the pie."

"For the pie? I thought it was all soup."

"A few of the nicest bits of meat mixed with potatoes make a beautiful pie, if you choose. The rest I put into the soup, with meal, or barley, or rice, some pot-herbs, a little pepper and salt, and let all simmer gently together for four or five hours more; and this will make two, or even three good dinners for us all. I allow three pints of water to every pound of stew, and, if properly cooked, I know whoever dines on that has what helps to keep him strong and hearty."

"Why, then, what with the soup, and the pie, and that nice jelly stuff you showed me the other day, made of the pickings of the bones, you have provision for four or five days."

"Yes, with vegetables, and rice or meal; and more too, sometimes, because I don't always give the children what I think good for their father; and then I like a change between. When fresh herrings come in, I do them all sorts of ways,—boiled, fried, potted, pickled, stewed,—for they're very cheap, and it's nothing but my own trouble, you know. They are wholesome when fresh, and are a nice change for William's supper, too. Sometimes we have a neck of mutton. The best part is done over potatoes at the bakehouse; the rest makes another dinner of meat, and perhaps two dinners of soup, — one day with herbs and meal, another day with split-peas. Pea-soup, you know, is very good when it's nicely made. I always take care to have herbs and vegetables as fresh as possible, greens especially, for they get unwholesome when they have been long cut."

"Well, I wish I could remember all this; for it shows how you must have been used to do things, Mrs. Taylor. You make nothing of the trouble."

"Indeed it's very little trouble, if I keep my things in place, clean and ready to use when they're wanted. It is a good plan to have a little rice, meal, barley, and such things in the cupboard. I buy a little whenever I can afford it, so that I haven't to run away from my work to get them at the shop just as I want to use 'them. That is always a sad loss of time, besides the chance of not giving time to cook them properly."

" You think a deal about that, I see," said Mrs. Freeman, thoughtfully. " Why, I've often given my poor children cold potatoes when I might have warmed them up, and only a crust of bread when, if I'd done right, they might have had a dish of comfortable soup. To tell you the truth, I hated the trouble, and thought it didn't matter if it only lasted through the day, and their stomachs were filled with something."

" But you think differently now, I'm sure," said Susan, encouragingly. " You see, if our bodies are to be kept alive by eating and drinking, it's our duty to do it the best way we can, and take proper care of our health when we've got it. Not long since, I thought I would do without any meat at all, and as little of everything so that I didn't actually starve; and I made excuses to William about it. But I found that, if I would work and be cheerful and industrious, it was of no use to stint myself of enough food, else there would soon be a doctor's bill to pay, besides the inconvenience to my family of being without my usual strength to do comfortably for them. It isn't economical to be ill if I can help it, I said to myself, and my husband likes best what we share with him. We are very careful, too, about the children and what they eat, and when, and how."

"Well, to be sure, I never thought to look after anything but setting it for them," said Martha. "Might I ask what you give them for breakfast and supper?"

"Porridge for breakfast, mostly, very well boiled, and sweet milk to it, and a slice of bread afterwards if they like."

"My children don't like it," said Martha; "sometimes it burns, and then they waste it."

"But it wont burn if it's attended to,— and it should be; for though very wholesome and nice made carefully, it is enough to make one turn from it when it's burnt, or only half boiled. I always boil it until it would turn out like a soft cake; and, either with cold milk or a spoonful of treacle, our children like it very much. They have a slice of bread and a cup of sweet milk for supper; or sometimes I boil the bread for them on cold winter evenings. They are never allowed to buy any of those nasty, cheap sweets, that so many poor children get sick with; but their halfpennies and pennies, when they have any, are kept for a better purpose."

"That's a good thought," said Martha. "I'll try to make my children do differently about that."

"You see, Mrs. Freeman, one of the things that it's right to look forward about is taking proper care of our children, body and soul. If we don't feed them the best way we can while they are growing, we've no business to be astonished if they get puny and rickety,

and grow up fit for nothing but to daw-
dle about and be a trouble to their
friends. I would rather patch their
clothes till you couldn't tell what they
were made of at first, than not give
them wholesome food, though it's ever
so plain, that they may be strong and
healthy men and women by and by. And
they should have their food, too, at
proper times, and in a proper manner.
Why, I've seen poor little things turned
out to the door-step to eat their bread
or porridge, just as you'd give it to a
dog or a cat, and no more thought
about the God who gave it than if they
lived in a heathen land."

Poor Martha's color rose, and her
eyes fell before Susan's earnest remark.
Full well she knew this was true of the

chief of the families in the street where she lived, and had been her own habit up to the present time.

"If I had only a crust of bread and a drink of water to give them," continued Susan, "they should come to it like Christians, and thank Him who can make it keep life and health within them, if it does not please him to give anything else to do it. Poverty is very trying, I know; but, if we make it an excuse for heathenish ways, and think it isn't worth while to sit down and thank God for our meal because it isn't as nice and plentiful as we should like, we are making it worse to bear, and teaching a bad lesson into the bargain."

"I suppose you don't give your children treats of nicer things when you can afford it," said Martha, "since you think only of what is wholesome."

"I can't bear eating and drinking treats," said Susan. "Children are naturally little gluttons, and if you help them to think about it you are encouraging a fault. I would rather they should think it a treat to go a walk with their father, or pick wild flowers in the fields, or do something kind and useful for somebody. But, if you mean, do I ever give them something they cannot often have,—I'm afraid I do, though only what is wholesome: a rice pudding, for instance, an apple dumpling, stewed rhubarb to their bread, or even an orange, when all such things are plentiful and cheap. I think God has given us everything in its season to use in moderation, and I would not have greedy eyes coveting tastes in secret of what I can give openly according to my means. I overheard little Robert one day, when a woman with a basket of oranges stopped near the door, and she asked him if he would like to buy one,—'No, thank you,' he said; 'mother can't afford it yet; when she can she'll give us some.' I felt then that my boy's confidence in my love and prudence was worth all I had ever done for him since he was born."

"Didn't you run and get him one that minute?" asked Martha.

"No," said Susan smiling. "I waited till they came down to the price that I thought right to give, and then they each had an orange more than once.

There's no good in making a merit of duty in young or old. Let us set before ourselves and our children the blessed principle of doing right for Christ's sake; and, though we know he honors them that honor him, we shall feel that, do the best we may, compared with what we ought, we are unprofitable servants still."

VII.

Shady Lane and Sunny Side.

BOUT six o'clock one summer evening a railway train stopped at the —— station, and out of a third-class carriage sprang three working-men, who began to scramble out as quickly as possible, two women, and some eight or nine children, with baskets, bundles and boxes, of all shapes and sizes. All being safely landed, the men rushed to the luggage-van, and another kind of load was less carefully turned out, consisting of sundry articles of furniture, which soon lay in a heap by the wayside. Then the guard held up his hand, the engine puffed, panted and screamed, and in another moment was off, leaving the travellers and their property to find shelter in a strange land.

"Mother, mother, where's our new home?" began one of the little ones, keeping fast hold of his mother's gown.

"Hush, child, I don't know yet. Be thankful we've all come safe," said she.

"We'll find a home presently," said one of the men, kindly patting the boy's head; "and you must make it a happy one by being very good to mother. See, I think this person is come to tell us where we're to go. Here, Freeman, Barnes," he continued, "you look after your families, and I'll see to the things there;" and William Taylor was met by a respectable-looking man, who said his cart was come to convey anything there might be to carry to the neighboring village.

"Your overlooker has got a poor woman to take most of you in till you see what to do with yourselves; so we'll go straight to her house," said he; and, smacking his whip, the little procession began to move on.

"Stop," he shouted again; "let the little ones ride if they like; lift them in, Ben, — there, I'll drive now myself;" and Ben, very much to his own satisfaction, jumped down to change places with his father. He was a country lad, and delighted to talk with the men from town, from whom he thought he could glean a little useful information.

By and by farmer Bates turned into a narrow winding lane, overhung on one side by tall trees backed by masses of foliage; on the other side stood several cottages, some together, some detached. "Here we are," said he, drawing up to the door of one of the cottages. "Now for some supper, little ones. This is Shady Lane, and here's Mrs. Brooks looking out for us."

A melancholy-looking woman in black came forward to receive the party, and after counting heads she declared that she could only find room for the women and children; the men must seek lodging elsewhere. "I reckon they'll be like to go to the 'public,'" said she; "there's nobody about here has got room, I'm afraid."

"Never mind about me," said William Taylor, hastily, "if you can just think of my friends here; perhaps we might ask the favor at some place in the village."

Farmer Bates scratched his head, wiped his brow, and looked thoughtful for a moment; then, clapping his hat down upon his head, "I have it," he cried; "we'll see what Dame Palmer can do. Come along with me, you," he said to Taylor; "and now give 'em some supper, Mrs. Brooks. I told my wife to send you a good can of new milk."

So while Freeman and Barnes unloaded, and put up their things in a shed, Taylor followed Mr. Bates to another cottage just beyond, where a rosy-faced, pleasant-looking woman was preparing the evening meal for her husband and son, who had lately come home from work. The farmer soon told his story, adding that as these men, none of them, liked staying at the "public," he meant to find room himself for two, if Mrs. Palmer could manage to accommodate the other.

John Palmer and his wife glanced quietly at the man who did not like staying at the "public." They had a spare bed; — yes, he who once slept in it sleeps in a narrower bed now; — it could soon be made up, and they could readily take Mr. Bates' word for the kind of guest he was introducing to them. So the matter was settled; and when the stranger ventured to speak for himself, he did so to such good purpose, that the honest couple decided he should seek no further for lodging as long as duty required his stay in the neighborhood. On the other hand, William Taylor rejoiced to find in Dame Palmer a friend whom he hoped to interest in the improving characters of Mrs. Freeman and Mrs. Barnes. Such a neighbor he thought would prove almost as valuable as his own good Susan; for a very short time sufficed to show how her skill and presence made "home" what it should be to those she loved.

But a new acquaintance demands a suitable introduction; and, as the reader cannot see that comfortable cottage and its cheerful mistress, a few words must picture them to the imagination.

Shady Lane was a pleasant walk in the glare and heat of a summer's day; but at most other times it was damp and cheerless. No sunbeams ever penetrated those tall trees to shine on the front of the cottages; but, as Dame Palmer wisely observed, the cottages had two sides as well as everything else, and those who loved sunshine could find it at the back, where it was light and cheerful nearly all the day long. And as for the trees, they were beautiful to look at; and moreover what shut out the sun, shut out also the keen east wind, which could do no more mischief than scatter a few leaves about.

There was a small room in front, which, if Mrs. Palmer had cared for " a parlor," might have made one; and when a lady, who knew and valued her as she deserved, made her a present of a Brussels carpet, just replaced by a new one, and a neighbor ventured to remark that of course she would put it into a parlor now, the good dame was seized with a merry little laugh at the idea. " What was the good," she said, " of a parlor to such as she ? It was only a show-place where nobody belonging to her would ever sit down as if it were home, and did for nothing but just for some stranger to shiver in a while, because the rest of the house wasn't fit to be seen." So the carpet, in spite of neighborly wonder as to whether the giver had any idea of its fate, was laid down every afternoon before the kitchen fire. The money that might have furnished " a show-place " was spent on substantial comforts for the kitchen; and the books that might have lain in dusty state upon a table were ranged on a shelf in the kitchen, as the mistress supposed they were printed to be read, and not merely to be looked at.

In short, there was no pretension about Mrs. Palmer. She was very thankful for the comforts with which her lot, she said, abounded, and made no struggle after appearances above her. In consequence, she never knew the pang of mortified pride or the sting of envy which distract the minds and disturb the peace of so many thousands in all ranks of life.

But in her zeal for the useful, had Mrs. Palmer no taste at all for the ornamental ? Bear witness a graceful fuchsia in the centre of the long window-sill, well sustained by a delicate dwarf rose, on either side a scarlet geranium and a musk plant. A venerable sampler in a black frame, with " the golden rule " worked in red, blue, and yellow, adorned the wall ; and amidst more useful articles on the mantle-shelf stood three conspicuous pieces of china, representing nymphs, swains, and peculiar-looking trees. These had belonged to a much-loved grandmother, and Dame Palmer daily wiped the dust from the ancient relics which renewed recollections of her happy childhood.

There was an easy-chair on one side of the fireplace for the good man; that is to say, no modern invention of

Master Ben running away from home to go to sea.   Chap. 10

springs and morocco, but high-backed oak, with stout stuff cushions, several other oak chairs with cushions too, polished tables, large and small, bright fire-irons, and the usual supply of pans and platters, all arranged in perfect order.

" Ah," suggests some housewife with four or five urchins trotting in and out of her untidy home, " there could have been no children to upset everything, and take up her time." Well, there were two daughters out at service, one son away in some foreign land, and another in the coal-pit with his father, and it is to be supposed they were children once; but everything in that kitchen is just as they remember it all their lives, save the Brussels carpet, and the renewed covers to the cushions ; and it was no bad sign that their great-grandmother's china and sampler had survived the natural propensities of young organs of destructiveness.

The back door, which opened at once from this pleasant kitchen, had a rustic porch with a seat on either side, commanding a foreground consisting of a neatly kept garden, with a box-edged walk leading to a brook which came dancing down from a neighboring hill bearing a message of refreshment to all who could look and listen. Beyond lay meadow lands, dotted with cattle, a wooden bridge, white houses peeping out from between clumps of trees, stretching away to a range of undulating hills.

But pleasant as was John Palmer's

cottage in itself, what would it have been to him without that dear, bright-faced "old woman," as he called her, whose presence was the charm of his home?"

"Old woman" it may be supposed was a pet term for a valued wife; for whatever Mrs. Palmer's age might be, very small trace of it was to be seen in the plump rosy cheek, the clear bright eye, and dimpling mouth of the active dame. Her hair was rather gray to be sure; but, as she indignantly eschewed black caps, there was no contrast to strike the eye between the smooth braid and the snowy border tied under her chin.

"Perhaps," suggests some faded matron, with a sigh, "perhaps she had passed happily through life without the cares and sorrows that make some of us prematurely old."

Nay, then, come to the village church-yard, and see there beneath the yew-trees' shade two little graves ; one headstone unites the two, bearing the names of "Ellen and John Palmer," one aged three, the other seven years; and close at their feet a longer grave, and another stone marked " Robert Palmer, aged nineteen," who, the inscription tells us, " fell asleep in Jesus." Say, mother, had not she who parted from these fair young buds, and that more fully blown flower, known sorrow, tears, and heart-wrenchings ? And again, another youth for aught she knew might be dead also; he had been away three years, and no tidings had comforted the loving hearts at home. Those on whose graves she drops the flowers on Sundays, she knows where they are, — safe at home forever; but of the wanderer she knows not anything, except that she prays for him, and prays to a prayer-hearing God.

Verily "the secret of the Lord is with them that fear him," and it is a secret that preserves very often health, and always peace, to them that treasure it. Trust in God through the Lord Jesus Christ, enjoyment of his pardoning love, and hope of his eternal presence, bore Mrs. Palmer up in all her sorrows; and, joined with obedience to that much-neglected precept, "Be content with such things as ye have," adorned her fair face with the sweet expression which gave pleasure to all who looked upon it.

It was a remarkable fact that many a trouble, brought in at the door from Shady Lane, by vexed or anxious neighbors, lost its keenness or bitterness on the sunny side of Dame Palmer's house, where sympathy was ready to soothe, advice to guide, and wise judgment brought to bear upon the case; so that it often assumed quite a different aspect, and either became possible to endure, or disappeared altogether under the calming influence of Christian truth and love.

"I will bless thee, and thou shalt be a blessing," was the promise to the patriarch of old; and in this, as in everything else, "the children of faith"

are sharers with "faithful Abraham."
"Blessed are the peacemakers; for
they shall be called the children of
God." And perhaps no characteristic
of his family is more needed or more
useful in humble life than this godlike
grace. May every working-man's wife
who reads of Dame Palmer, or is
favored to know one like her, seek just
such adorning as hers, and by and by
be just such a "dear old woman."

VIII.

The Bright Side and the Dark.

THE colliery district to which William Taylor and his companions were sent by their employer lay about half a mile beyond the wood that sheltered Shady Lane, and every morning a number of men bearing the complexion of the Anglo-Saxon race might be seen wending their way to work, and returning every evening black as a troop of savages, some dangling the empty cans which had contained their dinners, some carrying light branches for firewood, which, when useless for other purposes, were considered the laborers' perquisites. Happy the wife whose husband was thoughtful enough to come home thus loaded, and save her the unfeminine labor of getting it herself! When John Palmer and his son brought firewood, they took care also to chop it into pieces of a suitable size, and laid them neatly up in a corner of the garden handy for use.

Well did Dame Palmer know the firm step of her husband and the lighter one of her boy as they came round to the kitchen porch; and her smile of welcome was always ready as the two black faces popped in with a nod and a smile in return, and then disappeared to their dressing-room. Now, does any one laugh at the idea of a collier's dressing-room? It was a clever thought of the cleanly housewife, who, her husband said, "had no love for blackamoors except them that were born so," though she could better tolerate the coal-dust from below the ground than any manner of dust above it. "The dressing-room" was a small shed which had been made weather-proof and safe for the purpose, and furnished with great bowls of water, soap, and towels; and there, a few minutes before they were wanted, were placed two suits of well-aired every-day clothes, by which means two clean, cheerful-looking persons came forth to the home fireside, and their loving kiss left no black marks on the smiling lips that met them there.

William Taylor's company was no intrusion on a family glad to find in him a Christian after their own heart; and very thankful was he to sit down after his day's work was done and talk with them of " the loving-kindness of the Lord," taking "sweet counsel together" over John Palmer's great family Bible.

The youth, too, had taken a great fancy to him, and William thought he also was "not far from the kingdom of God." But he took care to make it very plain to the boy that "not far" was not within it, and that the decided step must be taken at the foot of the cross of Christ. *There* the most solemn view of "the' sinfulness of sin is got;" *there* the highest manifestation of the Father's love to sinners; and *there* hung the divine and human link by whom alone the holy and the fallen can be united in happy fellowship.

———

"I always think," said Mrs. Palmer, one evening, "what a mercy it is to see them come home safe, and no accident happened in the pit."

"So it is, Nelly," said her husband; "but you see there's no place nor calling without one sort of danger or another. That Mrs. Brooks, where your people are stopping," he added, turning to Taylor, "lost her husband a month ago on the railway. He used to say it was dangerous working in the pit,—he'd be in the open air; and one day as he stepped out of the way of one train, another that he didn't see ran over him, and he never spoke again. It was said he was a little in liquor, too; and, bad as it may be to die in a moment unawares like that, it's more awful to die unprepared."

"It is dangerous though in the pit, father," remarked Willy; "for you know one careless fellow might be the end of us all in no time."

"That's true, too, Will; but to hear the singing and laughing and swearing that sometimes ring through those black alleys, one wouldn't suppose there's any danger to body or soul among us."

"It's wonderful how the heart gets hardened by habit," said Taylor. "I thought, when I was down with you in your pit this morning, what a solemn thing it must be to work where, any moment, every human being there might be sent into eternity; and I felt as if I must ask every man I saw how it fared with his immortal soul. But some laughed, some scoffed, and said that was the way people talked who weren't used to it, and that the chances were as good for them as for me."

"And how did you feel for yourself?" asked Willy, inquisitively.

"I felt," he replied, "as I dare say your father does, that 'without God in the world' there is no safety anywhere, and with him real danger is nowhere, not even in a coal-pit; for to them that believe in the Lord Jesus Christ with true living faith, to be 'absent from the body' is to be 'present with the Lord.'"

"'It is God's providence that directed my calling, Willy," said Palmer, "and I hope yours too; for you know I haven't forced you to take to it; though I do say when the will runs the way of an honest living, it's a good thing for a son to work by his father's side."

"And I always mind that mother's praying for us every day, and nothing can happen before God's time," said Willy, meeting the fond mother's eyes, and feeling how happy it was to have such a mother. Happy mother to be loved and honored by an obedient son, and happy home where Christian peace presides, and faith sees "all things working together for good!" And when that faith is sorely tried, it is good to remember that "though it be tried with fire," it is that it may "be found unto praise and honor and glory at the appearing of Jesus Christ."

Among the business with which William Taylor was charged was that of seeing to the settling of his two fellow-workmen and their families in comfortable homes. Everything was to be done to afford them a fair beginning in life once more, and it was with great satisfaction that Taylor found the minister of the parish likely to feel interest in his new parishioners. The children were entered at the schools, and the poor widow Brooks having decided to leave her cottage, it was taken at once, in Mr. D——'s name, the families agreeing to live together until another became vacant, and relieve kind farmer Bates of his grateful lodgers. This was not the state of things Taylor was ordered to leave behind him; and, while he was fearing he would be unable to execute his employer's benevolent plan, an event occurred which made but too many cottages available for the purpose.

Many a scene of mourning, lamentation, and woe has passed in colliery life; and though in that class, as in all others, the Lord God has believing followers, beloved children, yet it is too sadly true that the risk of human life, and the terrible warnings so often seen and heard, seem utterly powerless to check abounding iniquity, and promote thoughtfulness, temperance, and industry. Holiday-making prevails to the inconvenience of business, and the detriment of family comfort and personal character; and the collier too often seems to think that he may indemnify himself for three or four days' hard and self-denying labor, by selfish and disreputable indulgence on his many voluntary holidays. The happiness of propping the door-post with a pipe in the mouth; talking and drinking in the ale-house, where the most influential opinions are those propounded by the man who can "stand treat" the longest; and playing at pitch and toss in the village street, — are not just the kinds of indulgence likely to elevate the character of the middle-aged, or improve the principles of the young. Suddenly some accident occurs, and a whole district is startled into thought, the drunkard refrains, a few days, from his glass, the swearer checks the curse in his speech, the Sabbath-breaker goes to church; but, the funerals over, the vacancies filled, all relapse again into old habits, as if there could be no more explosions, no more pit-floodings, no more treacherous machinery.

About two o'clock, one afternoon, a messenger in breathless haste dashed along Shady Lane. His gasped words struck dismay into every face he met, and, in a few moments, the lane was filled with distracted women and terrified children rushing toward the coal-pits.

An explosion had occurred, and brave men were hazarding their lives in hope to arrest some portion of the mischief. Several bodies were brought up in which life was not extinct, and, among the first, was poor Willy Palmer. His father, with desperate efforts, had saved him from suffocation, to be crushed with him, near the shaft, by a mass of falling coal.

There was a kind friend there to place the youth tenderly on the litter, and send him home at once; and, commending him to the mercy of God, William Taylor went back to seek the more injured father. John Palmer was respected by all who knew him, and many an anxious, kindly gaze was cast upon him, as he lay dying on William's breast.

"Can you bear to be carried home?" whispered Taylor.

"I am going home — to Jesus," was the faint reply. "Tell her, 'absent from the body, present with the Lord;' we shall meet again there by and by."

In the mean time, Mrs. Palmer, instead of flying along with her neighbor, on the first hearing of the terrible alarm, turned, sick at heart, into her cottage again, to ask for strength proportioned to her need, whatever it might prove to be. She strove to check the agony with which she saw her boy brought in, and her look of inquiry for her husband went to the hearts of his bearers. They hurried out again to make way for a surgeon, and fulfil some like errand to another bereaved home.

Willy's only cry was for his father while under the operator's hands, and his mother could not be spared to learn her husband's fate. Her thoughtful care was fully manifest in extremity like this; for, while in some of the houses not a scrap of old linen could be found, no warm water be had, nothing in its place when wanted most, her rolls of clean rags were at everybody's service, her kettle was in hasty requisition, her bed was smooth and ready; and the kind surgeon, understanding her deep anxiety, and admiring her self-control, released her as soon as possible, telling her that he would try to watch the son while she went to seek tidings of the father.

Soon she, too, was amidst the scene of sorrowful excitement, where, in utter self-abandonment piteous to behold, widows and children were beside their dead. Hers was not the wild paroxysm of ungoverned passion; her deep, true love, was chastened and sanctified by a still higher love, which, in this hour of anguish, bade her "trust and not be afraid." The heart that "is fixed, trusting in the Lord," seeks not to be "afraid of evil tidings" when they come, as come they must amidst the changes and chances of this mortal life.

As Mrs. Palmer sought among the crowd, her eyes fell here, on the drunkard, often warned, and cut down at last in his sin; there, the swearer with his oaths suddenly arrested on his lip; here, the indifferent and careless procrastinator, his good intentions at an end forever; and there, in blessed, peace-speaking contrast, the God-fearing Christian, his sorrows and wants and toils all over, his spirit fled to "the rest that remaineth." Freeman, one of the most active among the rescuers, saw the anxious face searching round, and kindly led Mrs. Palmer to the shed where William still supported his dying friend. Quietly and softly she took his place, thanking God in her heart that she had come in time for the last solemn moment. It seemed as if the spirit had lingered below for her coming. A smile, a gentle pressure of her welcome hand, an effort to whisper, " Peace in Jesus," and the soul of the Christian collier passed to eternal glory, leaving Dame Palmer " a widow indeed."

In due time the solemn duty was performed of committing "earth to earth, ashes to ashes, dust to dust," and a funeral sermon was preached to an attentive congregation. No more trying task could devolve upon a faithful pastor than that of discriminating for the living without seeming to judge the dead. "One event" had happened "to the righteous and to the wicked; to the clean and to the unclean;" in one sense, "as" was "the good" so was "the sinner," "and he that sweareth as he that feareth an oath." But with the grave-digger's spade the similitude ended. Sweet and precious consolation could be offered to those who sorrowed not without hope for the "blessed dead which died in the Lord." Even the grave had a sunny side for them, as they thought of "the spirits" before the throne of "just men made perfect." For the rest, the drawing aside of the curtain which veils their future will be all too soon, when the stupendous difference must be fully revealed between him that serveth the Lord and him that serveth him not. "He that believeth on the Son hath everlasting life ; and he that believeth not the Son shall not see life ; but the wrath of God abideth on him."

IX.

The Father's Chair.

ITTLE William Palmer lay upon his couch by the kitchen window, through which came the soft air mingling around him the scent of roses and musk. A small round table was at his elbow, on which stood his own little Bible and his late father's large one, in which he liked to look; for the texts often quoted by that dear father's lips, and out of which Dame Palmer had listened for so many years to the evening chapter, that it seemed to come out of it somehow more naturally than from any other.

Just by the couch sat William's cousin, Benjamin Bates, who had been sent the day after the funeral to see how he was going on; and Ben, having cultivated a very small stock of feeling for any one but himself, felt stupid and awkward, not knowing just what to say next. There never had been much congeniality between the youths, and now there was less than ever. At last Ben hit upon an appropriate idea.

" You wont ever go to the pit any more, I suppose, Will," said he.

" Yes I will," instantly replied William; " that is, I mean, if — if it pleases God to let me."

" Oh," said Ben with a laugh, " you needn't mind speaking that way before me. Aunt's not hearing you now, you know."

"No; but God hears me, and he knows best," said William, seriously.

"Well, if he cared about you, mayhap he wouldn't have let you get hurt so badly."

"It was to do me good, and it has done me good," answered William, warmly.

"You'll be telling me next it was good for poor uncle too, and he in the grave-yard," said Ben, half sneeringly.

"To be sure I shall. Why, do you think it isn't good to go almost in a few minutes straight to heaven to the Lord Jesus Christ? It is right good indeed for father; he's got the best of it all." And a bright smile played over Willy's face as his imagination attempted to picture the happiness in which he so evidently believed.

"Well," said Ben, "I know, if I was you, I'd never work in the pits any more. You're your own master now, you know."

"No, I'm not. I've given myself away."

"Given yourself away! What do you mean?" and Ben's eyes opened wide upon his cousin.

"Why, for one thing, if it pleased God to save my life, he's the best right to me,—hasn't he? Then it says in the Bible, 'Ye are not your own, ye are bought with a price.' Do you know what was given for me, Ben? 'The precious blood of Christ.' 'Therefore glorify God in your body and your spirit, which are his.' If God will let me do that, he can put me in the best place to do it, you know,—can't he?"

Ben did not know anything about it, and he felt impatient at it, too. " You're growing dreadful good," said he, after a pause.

" How are you growing, Ben, — upwards or downwards, eh? O Ben! be the servant of Jesus Christ, and he'll love you and take care of you forever. No real harm ever happens to them he loves."

" I don't see as you've any right to tell me that, lying here with a broken arm, and lots of bruises besides, and all just when you were doing your duty, I suppose," exclaimed Ben, out of all patience.

Then William lost his patience too, and forgot " the meekness and gentleness of Christ," while warmly defending the right of his Lord to do what he pleased with him; and his raised voice and quick words brought his mother down-stairs to see what was the matter.

"He's angry because I want him not to go working in the pits any more," said Ben, readily; so, gently advising William not to excite himself, she went back again.

"O Ben!" said William, "indeed that is not the truth; but I am very sorry I spoke so hard and fast to you. I know Jesus wouldn't have done it. It hurts me to hear you talk that way about him, Ben. I hope you'll love him yourself some time, and then you'll know how it is. But cousin, here "— and William dropped his voice to a whisper — "it isn't so much that I like the pits, but it's the best way for me to help mother; and I want that she shan't have to leave this cottage, where she's lived so many years, if I can do anything to help it.

Ben insisted upon it he should try some other way if he were his own master, and rose to go. William took his cousin's hand. "Ben," said he, "you'll forgive me for what I'm going to say, — wont you? Oh, if you will but believe me, ever since dear father's death I've remembered such lots of faults and things I did that must often have made him sorry, and it almost drove me mad, till Mr. Taylor read how 'the blood of Jesus Christ cleanseth from all sin,' and how God can forgive even such as I, though I haven't forgiven myself for all that. So I want to remind you,

11

Ben, to be good to your father and mother; you've got them both yet, Ben. Oh, if it was any use I'd give half my life this minute to have father here once more, that I might be a good son to him for the other half. But I've got mother yet, and please God I'll do it to her."

The tears filled William's eyes, and Ben, with a hoarse attempt at " Good-by," snatched away his hand and left the cottage. His cousin's words grated against his selfish inclinations, and he tried to forget them.

William thought that, when able to work again, he might venture to ask for man's wages now, and turned over in his mind every possible and impossible way by which to keep the cottage for his mother; but he knew very well that she would go anywhere, or do anything, rather than risk involvement, or shrink from the good pleasure of her heavenly Father, be his will what it might. So at last the anxious boy decided to give it up altogether into his hands, and felt calm and peaceful when, after a tearful struggle, he was able sincerely to say, " Not my will, but thine be done."

In the meantime it proved that one person's ·loss was another's gain; and while Mrs. Brooks gave up the cottage to Mr. Freeman and his family, another not less desirable, and vacated in consequence of a death by the late accident, became available for Barnes; and it was with feelings of delight that William Taylor executed the command of their employer, to provide the new homes with everything actually needful for decency and comfort.

The good work was but just completed when Mr. and Mrs. D—— and little Archy paid an unexpected visit to the scene of action. The latter, being a sort of privileged person, ventured a peep in at many a cottage in search of those he wanted. In some a group of children, obliged at times to realize something of their recent loss, stood about the widowed mother, who had already begun to wonder how she should find bread to supply so many mouths. Then a glance at the old Bible on the corner table reminded her of promises to the fatherless and the widow, and the little bird, as it twittered its good-night from the nest in the cottage eaves, seemed to rebuke the " little faith " of the tempted Christian.

Mr. Barnes had just seated himself with one child on each knee, and another before him with head erect, and hands behind, just as she was taught at school to say her evening hymn before her mother called them all to bed. An older girl, with a coarse apron tied round her little plump figure, was washing up the supper things, stopping every minute, or very slowly twirling the plate round with the towel, to hear how Polly was getting on. Mrs. Barnes, in a clean afternoon dress and tidy cap, sat by, seeming to be fitting an elbow-patch into a small jacket, but in reality thinking of her mended ways, her sober husband,

and once wild children thus fashioning
into civilization and knowledge, and
last, not least, the marvel that she
should have time and inclination to
put in that very patch. Why, she might
almost find time for a quiet talk with
Mrs. D—— herself nowadays. Her heart
was full of love and thankfulness; for
that was mended too, and was in fact
the greatest improvement of all; for
how could things go well with a sour
temper and a grumbling tongue?

Into this pleasant state of things suddenly popped the bright face of young
Archy, and while he asked the children
all about the new country life, the
grateful parents were displaying to their
benefactors the substantial comforts of
their orderly house. "We've never been

so happy in all our lives, ma'am, never before," warmly expatiated Mrs. Barnes. "Everything seems only too good for us."

"I don't think so, Mrs. Barnes," said Mr. D——, kindly. "I mean to see that every man that works for me has a comfortable home to begin with. If he and his can't keep it so, you know, hat wont be my fault."

"Sir," said Barnes, "I've been such a bad fellow, it's no use to let my tongue run about meaning to do better. I only hope you will see whether I am thankful or no for the lift you and my lady there have given us."

At Freeman's a no less gratifying change was visible; but William Tay-lor had other friends to introduce, and other tales to tell of sad and touching interest; and Archy, as he listened to that of the accident in his father's coal-pit, imbibed new interest in his working countrymen, and a new estimate of those comforts which their lives were daily per-illed to obtain.

On the next Sunday morning two members of the pastor's little flock re-turned thanks to God, who had in judgment remembered mercy, and the stifled voice of William Palmer whis-pered a sincere Amen. The widow re-membered that her husband, though dead to things temporal, was alive with Jesus forever more, and the mother knew that her son was "born again," an heir of the same blessed hope, and whether "living or dying," was now the Lord's.

On Monday, though not yet able for work, he could go out and see the overlooker, and ascertain his future prospect concerning it, and when he came in again his beaming face spoke eloquently of hope and pleasure. But Mrs. Palmer was not in the kitchen, and he sat down in his father's chair, which had stood vacant in its usual place ever since that sad day. William looked round him with mingled feelings of sorrow and joy, and regret and thankfulness, and then lost himself in a sweet vision of ministering love: — how he would work for and watch over his remaining parent; how he would deny himself to please and help her; how he would follow his father's ways, that she might fancy he was here again in the person of his son; and how he would ask God to make her happy, and let her feel that she had still an earthly, as well as a heavenly home. Thus occupied, he did not see her entrance until she stood gazing upon him with tears of gratitude for his recovery gathering in her eyes. Then he started from his seat, shocked that she should have found him in that chair.

"Stop there, my boy," said she, understanding it all. "Thy mother will like to see thee there; and, O William! if you follow him as he followed Christ, I have a dear treasure left me yet."

"Mother, it's all settled," Willy eagerly began. "My wages are to be raised. I've more particular work to do. And now we can keep our nice cottage. O mother, aren't you glad?"

"Very glad, very thankful, my dear son," said the mother.

"And, mother, it's all through Mr. D——'s kindness, and Mr. Taylor's telling him all about father and you. It was a good day that you took William Taylor in to lodge,—wasn't it? But now, mother,"—and the young man's voice softened and faltered,—"I want one thing, if you can do it: mother, dear mother, will you try to be happy again, something like you used to, and will it be like home to you now? I know father would like that it should be." And William's bent head drooped until it rested on her shoulder, and there he burst into tears.

It was a trying question, but the true-hearted mother would not for a thousand worlds have damped that filial wish. She struggled back the choking thought of widowhood that seemed to whisper, " No," to the idea of being happy at all as she " used to be ; " and, drying her tears, which fell plentifully over Willy's head, she lifted up his face, and smiled upon him one of the smiles he loved to see. " Yes, William," she said, " my dutiful, loving child can make happiness and home to me."

How sweet was William's rest that night ! A thankful mother's blessing on his head, and within his heart the approving voice of Him whose last act of earthly life was to provide a home and a son for the desolate mother who wept at the foot of the cross.

X.

Hopes and Disappointments.

HAT ho! hey, Master Ben, are you in too much hurry speak to to a friend?" exclaimed Barnes, as he was coming home from work, and Benjamin Bates sprang over a hedge close to him and was hastening along the lane.

"Oh, Mr. Barnes, beg pardon. I'm just going to ——, with this bundle of clothes for the tailor there to mend. Good-evening."

Barnes looked after him, his mind half inclining to an idea that Ben was about "no good." Why had he never mended that fence, of which he had been ten times told? .Why did he look so red and pale by turns even for the moment he paused? Barnes could not understand it. Alas! poor Ben was much more ready to break down fences than to mend them.

That evening farmer Bates had looked after the cattle and seen all safe before coming in to supper, and he came alone. "Where's Ben?" suddenly asked his wife.

"I don't know, I thought he was in. Oh, I remember I told him that fence in the far field must be mended at once, and he'd better do it before nightfall, else I must. Belike he'll come presently."

"Presently" passed away, and no Ben appeared. Mrs. Bates became fidgety, and rose to look out and listen every five minutes. Night settled down, and the little household looked anxiously in each other's faces to discern what thoughts might be seen there. Phebe, the only daughter, having said every-thing she could think of to account for Ben, suddenly took a new idea and went to her brother's room. She re-turned pale with agitation, and, sitting down, burst into tears.

"Don't fret, my girl," said her father, "or you'll grieve mother. May-be he's gone home with some of the lads after a game at skittles."

"Oh, no, father,—his clothes, his best clothes, all his things are gone."

"The ungrateful"— The father checked himself and looked at his pale wife. She was not in good health. This boy was her idol. How would she bear this blow? Unable to keep quiet, he reached his hat and thick stick, and trudged away to the village, to try if he could gather any tidings of Ben.

One farmer Watts was just finishing his pipe at the door in the moonlight as the anxious father came by. Hearing the news he turned in and called up the stairs to his sons who had just gone to their beds. " Jim, Will — here's a pretty kettle of fish! Ben Bates is gone off, nobody knows where. Hast seen anything of him? "

" No, father," answered Jim; "but I can guess what's up with him. I dare say he's gone off to sea at last; he's often said he should some day."

"Whew! never mind then, neighbor Bates; a good sea-storm will bring him to; and he'll come back all the better for it one of these days. If I was you I'd let him alone."

"He's never been settled since Joe Willis went away in his blue jacket and straw hat, to be bound on board the 'Water Witch' for New Zealand," called out Jim again.

"Ho! and mayhap some more of our foolish chaps aren't going to be settled now that Ben's gone after the blue jacket and straw hat to nobody knows where."

"Well that an't me, father. I'd sooner live a-top of our rick than be tossed about in the biggest ship as ever sailed, only"—for Jim thought this was a capital opportunity to say what he did wish — "I want to see London, that's all."

"Thou shalt see London some day, if thee's a good lad; there be cheap ways of doing things now, that made one's hair stand on end to think on when I was young." And very well satisfied with the extent of his son's ambition, Mr. Watts, notwithstanding his advice to farmer Bates to let the boy alone, kindly followed him to offer the use of a horse, if he meant to try and overtake him.

Bad news flies fast; and, though it was getting very late, Barnes, who could give a little information, and Dame Palmer, who could at least give sympathy, were soon on their way to the farm, where they found Phebe and her mother, the picture of heart-sorrow, cowering over the embers of a fire.

The loving heart of the happier mother was touched to the core; but she knew where patience and comfort, even in such a case as this, might be sought and found. Mr. and Mrs. Bates too knew something of the refuge,

> " From every stormy wind that blows,
> From every swelling tide of woes ; "

but they seemed to have lost sight of it just now; and it was blessed to hear of it in the reminding voice of one so lately tried herself with deep affliction. So they knelt down together and commended the boy to the pity, protection, and forgiveness of Him whose " eyes are in every place beholding the evil and the good;" and they found, as all do who try and trust, that "God is our refuge and strength, a very present help in trouble."

Meantime the young truant, who, in reckless pursuit of his own way, had thus quitted his comfortable home, and left his best earthly friends to consume the hours in sickening suspense, was flying along by rail to a large seaport town, where he arrived with all his worldly goods in a bundle, and his money-savings in his pocket, a stranger from the country, ignorant of the ways of the classes around him as he stared about from pier to pier, wondering which of the grand ships, that lay in stately calm upon the river, was destined to realize his boy-dreams of the wonderful sea.

Two sailors lounging along to their ship saw his eager and excited looks, and soon accosted him. The acquaintance resulted in an engagement with their captain to take him to sea; and they in the meantime volunteered their help in showing him something of the world on shore, — the low world about the docks and shipping of a great commercial port. More than once Ben thought of his country home, and what his parents would think could they see him now; but he seemed to forget all they might suffer because they could not see him, nor know whither he was gone.

The captain liked his appearance. He asked no questions, for he knew that many a bad youth has his own bad reasons for quitting home; and he had

such confidence in his own talents as a
disciplinarian that disobedient sons, or
dishonest apprentices, or whatever else
they might have been, disobedient sailors none under him should dare to be.

It was on the third evening after
Ben's disappearance that his depressed
and anxious mother, after a half day's
journey, found herself in the neat and
humble home of William Taylor, tenderly commended by him to the care
and sympathy of his good Susan. She
had followed her husband in the hope
that she might see her boy once more
before he went to sea, if indeed he were
yet on shore at all. This was the
second day of the father's search; for
the clew had been supplied in the questions put by Ben to Barnes from time

to time concerning the neighborhood of the docks in his native town; and it was resolved that every public-house, and every sailor's store should be examined before the cause was given up.

How and where he laid his hand upon the shoulder of his startled son, farmer Bates did not think proper to tell, as he brought the youth that evening into his mother's presence; but, as she held him once more, and looked lovingly in his face, she felt there was yet a deeper depth of sorrow in store if he had taken to drink, for the fumes of liquor were burning in his breath.

"We are not come to hinder thee from the sea, Ben," she whispered; "but oh, my son, thou hast broken thy mother's heart!'

The captain and Ben being both re-solved to stand to their engagement, it was legally made and witnessed, and the boy was suitably fitted out for sea from his father's savings. The father gave up his cherished wish to have a son at home to assist him in his work, and cheer his declining years; the mother surrendered her idol to the life he pre-ferred to her and duty, and nothing remained but to see him sail.

The ship was delayed a week longer, and day by day they walked the piers, or sat on some temporary resting-place watching her from morning till night. On the last two days they were accom-panied by a young woman with an infant in her arms, and this was Ben's eldest sister, who had travelled all the way from London to see once more the cherished pet of her early years.

Ben must have been made of stone to resist the softening influence of all this family affection. At last he did seem to feel it, and to think that he did not quite deserve it. His mother seized the moment to ask a promise that he would read the little Bible she had put among his things. "There will be nothing else to remind thee of home," she said; "and if thou forget God, who shall speak a word for him?"

They were just about to part. The ship had moved out of dock into the river, and a boat was waiting to convey back those who had been allowed as a special favor to take a last leave on shore. A sailor stood near as the words were uttered; and coming closer to the little group he took off his cap and quietly said, " Mistress, I fear God; and your lad shan't want a reminder of him while I'm spared to speak it."

Oh, how quickly that sailor's rough hands were clasped in theirs! What a load of anxiety seemed lifted from their hearts in the assurance that at least one God-fearing seaman was among the crew!

Before nightfall the watchings were over; the ship passed down the river, became a speck in the horizon, and soon danced on the waves of the western main.

Thus Benjamin Bates secured his heart's desire in his own hard-hearted, ungrateful way. He regarded not the love that had watched over him for fifteen or sixteen years; he heeded not God's command, " Honor thy father and mother ; " he fancied he came into the world to do as he pleased, and in so doing scrupled not to trample on the first claims of human duty. It was not his place to chasten a father's pride, or a fond mother's over-indulgent affection ; and though this might follow, as good out of evil often does, yet that was not within his province, and the responsibility of his sin must be on his own head.

If the statistics of human sorrow could be gathered and examined, it would probably be found that bitterer tears have been wrung from aching hearts through the selfishness and disobedience of children, than by the desolations of death, the cares of poverty, or the pangs of sickness. "How sharper than a serpent's tooth it is to have a thankless child!" The solemn displeasure of Almighty God rests upon "despisers of fathers and mothers;" and the "disobedient and unthankful," and "without natural affection," occupy a fearful prominence in the predictions of future judgment. Home, in whatever rank of life, should be, to every inmate, a spot sacred to love and duty; and woe to him who dares to mar its peace with headstrong will and selfish passions! Much is said and thought about parental responsibility; but let not children forget their share in the great account.

"Mother," whispered little Robert in his mother's ear, "why do they cry so sadly? Is it because Ben has gone to sea?"

"Not entirely, Robert; more because of the way he took to go. Tears may often come for an absent son, and they will be wiped away; but the tears that come for a disobedient, ungrateful son, O Robert! I'm afraid they flow on always on this side of the grave."

"O mother!" and Robert put his arms round his mother's neck. "I'll remember this, and pray to God that you may never shed such tears for me."

As Susan held her son to her thankful heart, she could not help following in imagination the farmer and his wife to their altered home; and her feelings did not exaggerate the reality. A hoped-for prop was gone. Everything seemed changed; and it was hard for a daughter's thoughtful love to fill her own and her absent brother's place. The father strove manfully, as fathers do, to conceal his disappointment, and make the best of what couldn't now be helped; and the mother drooped and suffered meekly, as mothers do when the wound is at the heart, and sweet hopes are dashed to pieces by the hand least expected to inflict the blow.

XI.

A Time to Sow, a Time to Reap.

AVING seen his reformed fellow-workmen comfortably settled according to the wishes of their employer, William Taylor returned home to the quiet, steady fulfilment of his own immediate duties. Business prospered, the rate of wages was satisfactory, and all things went on happily for some time.

One day Mr. D—— came from his office, looking somewhat perplexed, and calling his son, who had just come in from school, "Archy," said he, "try and help me to find out what is to be done in a difficult matter."

" What is it, papa ? " exclaimed Archy, now a strong, fine boy, as he hastened to his father's side.

"Are you willing to part with your friend William Taylor ? "

" No indeed, papa, that I'm not, nor with Robert either. I want Mr. Taylor to be with you when I come to learn the business."

" So do I, Archy. But I have received a letter to-day from his old masters, inquiring all about him. They want him back again; for he was faithful and resolute to stand by them when their men struck for wages; and, now that they are prospering again, they wish to reward him with a better

Mr. Barnes advising Ben to quit the Sea. Chap. 10.

situation, and prove that they appreciate his worth. I honor them for this: it is as it should be."

" Yes, papa; but surely you will not let him go. You can't spare him; for we know his worth as well as they do."

" True; but we must not be selfish, nor stand in the way of his real interest. Perhaps it is his duty for his children's sake to accept so good an offer."

" Oh, I hope not! What shall we do, papa? I wish I were a man."

" How would that help us out of our difficulty, I wonder?" said Mr. D——, smiling on the earnest boy. " What would you do, Archy? Perhaps I, being a man, can do it for you."

" Why, I would tell him how I love and trust him. I would say I have

known you ever since I was a little
boy, and I want you to stay and take
care of my business, and your son shall
learn it too; and I'll build you a
house, and you shall be my friend
always; and, if I can, I'll give you more
money than those people will; and
when you are old I will take care of
you if I live too."

"Well done, Archy. I am very much
inclined to leave this affair in your
hands. With regard to Robert you may
promise for me; the rest you know is
all your own. But you may add this
in my name: 'William Taylor, you
have made many friends among us.
Drunkards have become sober men under
your influence, and miserable homes
have been made happy and comfortable.

Your character and example have been useful to all, from the master to the humblest workman in the yard. Your wife is a blessing among our women; your well-trained children are a credit to your care; and though you may do and be all this elsewhere, we wish to keep you with us to do greater things.' "

" May I, shall I, papa? Oh, how glad I shall be to say it all ! "

" Then you shall take the letter to Taylor's house this evening; and I will come for you, and hear how my young ambassador has prospered in my cause."

Archy's bright face was always welcome at William Taylor's cottage; and the occasion of his present visit brought him bounding in with more than usual speed. He was at the age which hopes

———

everything, and when the idea of disappointment seldom comes to blight the pleasures of anticipation.

William came forward to receive his young visitor, as he never could help doing, with paternal interest; and Robert kept his hand with something of admiration and love, blended with a respectful remembrance of their relative positions in life. The two sons of employer and employed had long felt an interest in each other, which was growing with their growth, and while on one side there was no ground for fear of " evil communications," on the other there was the self-respect that shunned intrusion, and frankly accepted the token of present good-will, without a calculation upon anything beyond it.

"Papa sent this letter for you to read, Mr. Taylor," said Archy; "and I want to tell you that I hope and papa hopes you wont go, but stop here and do more good. We love you so much,— indeed, indeed you must not go away."

William took the letter in surprise; Susan ceased plying her needle; Robert looked from one to the other in great amazement; and Archy, with his elbows on the table and his chin on his hands, watched William's countenance as he read, and then handed the gratifying letter to Susan.

"Now, Robert, ask your father not to leave us, and we'll all be so happy. You and I shall grow up together to learn papa's business, and we shall always be friends, you know; and, Mr.

Taylor, I was to tell you this from papa." And then he repeated with commendable accuracy what his father had said, until tears gathered in William's eyes, and his head drooped over the wondering boy's, who had drawn closer to him.

Mr. D—— soon arrived, and, while Archy drew Robert to the window to look over a new book he had brought to show him, the two parents sat down to talk over their views together.

" Sir, dear master," said William, " I am not able to thank you enough for your great kindness."

" There's no need to thank me, Taylor, for wishing to keep a good servant when I find one; but I know it is your duty to consider what is best for your family, and I must not venture to persuade. Think over both sides of the subject for a day or two, and then let me know your decision."

"Thank you, sir. It is written, 'In all thy ways acknowledge God, and he shall direct thy paths.' I trust he will do so now, and teach me to do his will."

"You'll stay," cried Archy, as his father called him to walk home; "you'll stay with us, — wont you?"

"If it pleases God," whispered William, as he bade his young friend good-night.

Archy turned back again to look at Robert, who stood leaning against the window-frame, unusually quiet. "He's not well, Mrs. Taylor," said Archy.

"See how pale he looks. I wonder what's the matter with him."

"I'll go to bed, please, mother; it's only a headache," said Robert. "Good-night, dear, kind master Archy. I hope we shall stay with you."

Robert went to bed, and then the husband and wife talked long together, and laid the letter with all their feelings about it before the throne of grace. Many had been their privileges and their pleasures in that former home, and Susan's dear parents and other relatives were not forgotten among the inducements to return. But it seemed to them that a sweet and powerful bond united their hearts to William's present employer and his family, and that God's blessing had assuredly rested upon their humble efforts to spread a holy influence around them. It was true that Mr. D—— could not make the wages equal to those offered in the advanced situation; but his kind attentions toward Robert were not to be disregarded; and should they for a few pounds more a year quit the service of one by whom they were thoroughly valued, and to whom they were justly attached in return? Once the thought crossed the father's mind that those few pounds would enable him to send Robert to a higher school, and give him a chance of advancement in life by superior education. But he banished it with the better remembrance that the son of a working-man, who was to be in his turn a working-man too, should be educated in and for the position in which God had placed him; and any future elevation should be the result of an overruling Providence, and not the coveted aim of parental pride. Still, gratitude for the kindness of his former masters, and a thorough satisfaction with their conduct in the matter of "a strike," made him hesitate whether it was right to reject their generous offer. William laid his head on his pillow still undecided, and Susan feared to influence, lest her own will should in any respect be tempting her to misinterpret the wiser will of God.

The next morning brought with it new and unexpected subjects of anxiety. Poor Robert's headache became alarming illness, and when Archy looked

in at midday, on his way from school,
he was shocked at the change in his
young friend. He hurried home to beg
his kind mother to go and see if she
could do him any good. Mrs. D——
was not long in fulfilling this request;
and, when medical opinion declared the
case a dangerous one, she took the two
little girls to her own house, and feared
not to see them among the precious
occupants of her nursery, where truth
and love and obedience were much more
highly prized than all temporal distinc-
tions. Nothing was neglected, that occurred to human skill and thoughtful
love, 'for the young sufferer's benefit,
and in the affectionate concern and attentions of Mr. and Mrs. D—— was
found a sweet return of all that had

been felt for them under somewhat similar circumstances. So true it is that "with whatsoever measure ye mete, it shall be measured to you again;" and truly here was "good measure, pressed down and running over."

Three times a day did young Archy visit the cottage, forbidden to see, but earnestly inquiring for, his favorite, and catching from Susan's countenance the hopes and fears of a trying season of suspense. Often the parents knelt by the little bed, seeking for grace to resign their darling willingly to his heavenly rest, meekly acknowledging the right of Him who gave to take away, and struggling to realize love in both the gift and the privation. And they were not the only parents who have attained their triumph, and then received, back from the very gate of death the loved one by whose pillow the battle has been fought.

At last the crisis passed, and the doctors gave hope of recovery with continued care and good nursing; and Archy was permitted to look again on the pale, thin face of the once robust, blooming boy. That look seemed to rivet the two young hearts more firmly together.

"Dear Robert," whispered Archy, "God has not taken you away, and your father must not."

"No, he has promised," said Robert, pressing Archy's hand against his thin cheek. "Thank you for loving me, dear, dear master Archy."

"I have been wondering whether you would see it right to accept the opportunity of taking Robert back to his native air," said Susan' to her husband.

"Oh, no, dear wife; he must have change, but not that way. I am bound to Mr. D—— by ties that cannot be broken. No wages, no situation, could ever be to me what he has been in this time of sorrow." So, with explanations and apologies for the delay, William's respectful letter of thanks, expressive of his satisfaction in his present service, was placed in Mr. D——'s hands, and duly forwarded to its destination.

At the same time Susan wrote to her former kind friend and district visitor, Mrs. Ashton, asking her to use her influence in behalf of Richard Moore, who was, she trusted, thoroughly steady and trustworthy now, and of whose improved home and family she heard cheering accounts from her mother. The application was successful, and, Richard Moore, to his own and Betsey's great thankfulness and delight, obtained the situation.

XII.

Friends and Foundations.

THE day on which William Taylor's decision was made to remain in the service of his present master, Mr. D—— took a drive with his family to look at a house he had recently taken a few miles out of town, and whither he proposed removing as soon as certain improvements were made. It was near to a railway station, and a few minutes would effect communication between home and his place of business, whenever Mr. D—— chose to avail himself of the trains. "It needs now a sort of lodge at these gates," said he as he drove into the grounds, " and I intend to build one. I requested the foundation to be got ready that Archy may lay the first stone to-day."

Archy was highly delighted at this honor, and performed his part amidst the eager interest of his little brothers and sisters. " Will it be like the lodge at Beech House, papa, — two tiny rooms, with roses round the porch ? "

" No, there will be a comfortable parlor, and kitchen and wash-house, with three airy bedrooms over them, according to my plan. It will face the road, and the little garden will be behind those trees. As for the roses round a porch at the door, I have no objection to your training as many as you please."

Archy supposed a gardener would live there, so his taste in roses might be easily gratified.

Some time afterwards Mrs. Hayes paid a visit to William and Susan, to assist the latter after a fourth child had been added to the youthful group; and very acceptable was her kind and active help. "Never mind, my dear," said she, one day, after procuring some comfort, which Susan had refused herself as beyond her husband's means. "When God sends more mouths, it's a sign he's got some way ready to fill them, and the mother is not to be forgotten in the self-denying wife." So Susan had to submit to her kind aunt's thoughtful indulgences.

Mrs. Hayes' idea of "signs" was not

to be despised; and when, after she had carried off Robert to recruit his strength and restore his faded bloom at the farm, — a thing impossible she said in that huge, smoky town, — she would not consent to be surprised at some very good news which followed her.

One morning there was a little stir and excitement among the men in Mr. D——'s premises. They were grouped together as they had been once before when making their request concerning the place and time of paying wages; but it might have been observed that on this occasion Taylor was not among them.

It had become known that the foreman of the yard was about to resign his situation in consequence of other prospects elsewhere, and, though the men liked him, they were just now think-ing more about the choice of a successor.

"I wish master would take a word from us about it," said one.

"Well, it an't likely, you see; we might just as well each elect himself," said another, laughing at the conceit; "and there isn't one of us fit for the place, after all; it needs a deal of judg-ment and impartiality to be foreman over a lot of fellows like us."

"There's one man among us I'd like to see in the place, howsomever," re-plied the first speaker; and as Mr. D—— came in, he was respectfully asked if a new foreman were engaged.

"Not yet my good friends," said Mr. D——, kindly. "I am a little more par-ticular than I once was, and I want to find a man whom you will all respect."

"We could soon find him, sir, if we might."

"Then, come, any of you, and give me your opinions privately," said Mr. D——, both surprised and pleased; and in less than ten minutes the name of William Taylor had been uttered in the office by three fourths of his fellow-workmen.

"And why William Taylor?" asked Mr. D——.

"Well, sir, he's so steady and straightforward, you see; and though we've never caught him tripping in anything, there's no pride nor self-righteousness about him; and he's a real help when one gets cast down a bit, or feels idle and discontented like."

"That's true enough," said another,

he's been the saving of me and mine from drunkenness and starvation; and many's the bother I've given him, trying to make me do my duty."

"And see how Freeman and Barnes owe pretty nigh everything to him, saving your presence, sir," exclaimed a zealous friend to both. "Why, Freeman was over last holiday to see his old mother, and she scarce knew him with his fine, healthy face and pleasant ways; and he says Barnes is getting on just as well; and I asked him how it came about, and he put it in the right place when he said, 'It's just God's goodness, and Will Taylor.'"

Very pleasant it was to Mr. D——— to witness this right feeling towards one in every way superior, and he had no hesitation in confirming the honorable choice. William was, or very soon could be, quite equal to his new duties, and, with three cheers for the master, and a right hearty one for the foreman-elect, the men went off like a set of overgrown boys, to find and congratulate him on the subject.

"Before honor is humility." The humble-minded, contented working-man, quietly struggling through difficulties, meekly bending to the providence of God, resisting temptation to consider earthly advantage before the claims of gratitude and love, had been under discipline preparatory to a right reception of honor when it came; and, whatever the second causes, He, "from whom cometh every good and perfect gift," had the first thankful acknowledgments of his right-hearted children.

The foreman had given Mr. D—— ample notice, and, ere he resigned his duties, the family had removed to the house in the country, the lodge was completed, and Mr. D—— found an errand for William Taylor into the coal district, where he contrived to have him detained for two or three weeks. The good report of Freeman and Barnes was pleasantly confirmed. Mrs. Palmer and her excellent son were still in their comfortable cottage, and, so far as could be judged by the placid face and thankful expressions of the widowed mother, the loving desire of her child was as fully granted as it could be on this side the grave.

Taylor returned home one afternoon towards Christmas time, and was greatly astonished to find his house shut up, and no smiling faces as of old peeping out to greet him. In much perplexity he stepped back to survey the upper window; but no sign of life was there, and with rising fear and anxiety he was about to apply at the next door for information, when Mr. D—— came up in the light carriage which often brought him into town.

"I went to meet the train, but it was in, so I drove after you, Taylor," he said, as he checked the horse.

"Sir, what has happened? where are they?" gasped William.

"All safe and well, only gone for a little change of air. I hoped to have saved you this needless anxiety; but come, jump in, bundle and all, and we'll be with them directly."

"Thank you, sir," said William, gladly obeying. "The house looks so desolate, I thought my family could scarce be in it."

Away they went, through the suburbs, out of town, along a pleasant road, stopping at last before a building, which was neither quite a cottage nor quite a house, with white blinds and muslin curtains. A little court in front was laid with turf, out of which were cut flower-beds planted with evergreens.

"Are they lodging here, sir?" asked William, in much surprise, as several heads were seen watching between the curtains, and whence an evident rush took place to the door.

"This is my new lodge, Taylor," said Mr. D——, "and I want it kept in good order, inside as well as out, — so that, as I come in at my gate every day, I may have the pleasure of seeing here a reflection from my own fireside, and pass on to enjoy my home blessings the more for knowing they are shared in kind by you."

There was no time for any more staring with wide-opened eyes on Mr. D——, for a welcoming group of happy faces pressed round the dumb foreman. There was Susan with tears in her eyes, and a smile on her lip; there was Robert with roses again in his cheeks, and health in his sparkling eyes; there was Milly, and the ex-baby, all frantic with joy; and there was Mrs.

D—— in the background, holding the young reigning tyrant while the mother went to receive her husband; and there was the hearty grasp of Jonathan Hayes and his prophetic dame, unable to find any words, because, as he said, it was quite too much for him altogether.

And Archy, the honest workman's first friend in the family, he was there, too, his young heart bursting with a strange mingling of many happy thoughts, and ready to whisper in broken voice his own welcome in William's ear : — " This is your home, and Robert's home; and we are all so glad to see you here. You'll be happy here, — wont you now ? "

"Welcome home, my friend, and may

God bless you all," said Mr. D——. "Come, Archy, don't forget that the traveller wants some dinner;" and Mr. and Mrs. D—— hastily escaped from the acknowledgments that were trembling on William's lips.

"Only a word more," whispered Archy, pulling him toward a table in the window, on which stood a handsome family Bible. "This is my present, William. We thought you would like it better than anything else. You'll read in it to-night, — wont you?" And, slipping from the answering clasp of William's arms, the happy boy flew after his parents, leaving the reunited family to enjoy, as they might, the present reward of faith and duty.

On the whole, the experiences of life,

the records of history, and even "the annals of the poor," prove that piety, industry, and sobriety are the best capital on which any man can start on the business by which he is to earn his daily bread. There is no path of either usefulness, respectability, or honor closed against such in our free and highly favored land; and, while there is scarcely an office known to our government that has not been held by working-men, the history of commercial and manufacturing life affords still more ample evidence of the scope and opportunity open to all. Often may be seen the trustworthy servant a master and employer in his turn; often the sons of master and servant stand side by side on the "exchange" and in society, equal in talent and enterprise, and friends for life.

But this belongs to the external scene. Where is the working-man's rest from toil, and the best earthly sympathy in all his cares and trials? Where the child's most watchful guardian and influential friend? Where, but at " home, " in the industrious, loving wife, the prayerful, tender mother, quietly, meekly, in the strength of God, filling her appointed place, where love and duty constitute her praise. Show me such wives and mothers, and I will show where lies the guaranty of a nation's prosperity and strength, and the assurance of God's blessing on " HOME IN HUMBLE LIFE. "

THE KING'S MESSENGER.

(225)

The King's Messenger.

JEFFRY HAYES was a person of considerable importance in his little neighborhood; for not only was he the champion of every malcontent who braved a quarrel, and resolved to fight it out with the offender, but he had the first and surest news in days when armed horsemen did the work now performed by rail and telegraph, and when gossips bursting with impatience rushed to the blacksmith's forge to hear from his lips the last report left behind by some galloping rider who had been detained while his horse was shod.

Jeffry did not fail to make the most of such opportunities; and at a time when insurrection had disturbed a portion of the king's dominions, he was in the height of village popularity, dispensing news and leading politics, and enjoying the well-earned distinction of being known as the best craftsman of his kind, and the most loyal, to be found on the great London road.

One dark evening as usual the bright fire from the smithy of Jeffry Hayes flung its ruddy glow across the highway; the sounds of labor had ceased, and several idle villagers were lounging round their oracle until he should think proper to put out his fire, and adjourn with them to the nearest ale-house. The smith himself, with broad shoulder and muscular arm, was flourishing his great hammer to the eager narrative of an angry youth, who was telling of an insult he wished to avenge, and was enlisting the pugnacious sympathies of his athletic friend, who praised his courage, and promised all honorable assistance on the occasion.

"Ay, I was sure you would stand by me, and see justice done," said the obliged challenger.

"That will I," said Hayes warmly, and with various oaths. "Fix time and place, and I'll be there to the minute, if the high sheriff himself, on his majesty's errand, brought his horse to be shod as no one but Jeffry Hayes can do it.

I'm not the man, as you all know, to desert a friend in need, nor keep out of the way when blows are going. But hark! here comes a horseman, and I hear by the foot-fall there's work to be done yet. Stand by, my lads, and let the gentleman ride straight in."

In a few seconds more a horseman rode up, and asked if a lost shoe could be replaced at once.

"Just in time, sir," said Jeffry, stepping forward, and lifting the hoof, while the rider dismounted, and, leaning against the door-post, surveyed by firelight the several persons in the shed.

"You've ridden hard and far, sir," said the smith, as he proceeded to work.

"Yes; and must further still before I rest," replied the stranger.

"Important business on hand, I suppose, sir?" said Jeffry.

"Very. I am a King's messenger, and must not loiter on my way."

If hammer could speak, that of Jeffry Hayes would have borne witness to the right loyal grasp of its master's powerful hand, as he swung it with increased vehemence and precision on hearing this.

"Good news at court, I hope, sir," said he, pompously.

"The very best. A free pardon for all the rebels."

"A free pardon!" exclaimed all at once. "What, after all they have said and done?"

"Free, unconditional pardon," repeated the traveller, "except it be considered a condition that they accept it."

"They can't, surely, but do that," exclaimed Jeffry. "The very thought of such clemency ought to make them lay down their arms, and be true subjects for the rest of their lives."

"Yet, strange to say, the fact, though quite certain, does not do it."

"What, are they going on in rebellion in the face of pardon, and with no hope, either, of success at last?"

"Even so, excepting here and there one who sees things in a better light."

"Well, then, they deserve execution; and why should not justice take its course?" said the blacksmith, fiercely. "My opinion is that it's possible to be too lenient; and loyal men look to governments to do their duty without fear or favor."

"You would have me believe that you are not a rebel yourself, friend," said the stranger in a low voice to the smith.

"I! Yes, I would like to see the man who dares call me rebel," said Jeffry Hayes, with the voice of a Stentor, and mingling his speech with many terrible oaths; "he should know something of this arm." And down came the hammer upon the anvil with a blow that made the roof ring again.

"Then that dare I," said the traveller, boldly; "and your own lips have condemned you."

"You had better mount and be gone," whispered a villager, at the sight of Jeffry's face, like a thunder-cloud, as he slowly lifted himself from bending over the horse's hoof, and fixed a flashing eye on the stranger's face, who neverthe-less stood unmoved and undismayed, adding, deliberately, —

" ' Thou shalt not take the name of the Lord thy God in vain; for the Lord will not hold him guiltless that taketh his name in vain.' So runs the holy law, and I call you all to witness that no loyal man trifles with or profanes the name of the prince he loves and serves. How say you, friends, — is it not rebellion against God, wilfully and continually to break and despise his law?"

There was no answer, and Jeffry was busy with the shoe again.

" But," continued the stranger, " I told you that I am the King's messenger, bearing unconditional free pardon to all who will accept it. All have sinned; all are rebels; but God, who is rich in mercy, 'so loved the world, that he gave his only begotten Son, that whosoever believeth in him should not perish, but have everlasting life.' Is it not enough to silence the blasphemous tongue, and make him reverence the God who loves like this? Will you accept free pardon, and act out your own views of its consequences, my honest friend?"

"Why ask only me? There be others here who need it fully as much," said the smith, in a surly tone.

"I do say it to all. 'Whosoever will, let him take the water of life freely.' I have no reserves on my list, but, according to my royal Master's will, I repeat his own proclamation to every sinner, — 'He that believeth on

Him that sent me hath everlasting life, and shall not come into condemnation.' "

" I thought you were on an errand from the real court, and not making up a tale to preach to us," said Hayes, with some remaining displeasure.

" It is no made-up tale; it is solemn truth, as you will one day prove; and as God the King of kings is real, as heaven and hell are real, as you, an immortal being, are real, I beseech you, as though God himself besought you. by me, receive his offers of pardon and grace, and be reconciled to him. No man who is reconciled to God talks as you talk. Of deeds and ways I know nothing; but your own conscience will tell you whether you live and speak and act like a follower of the gentle, loving Saviour."

"Your horse is shod, sir."

"I thank you heartily for good speed and good work," said the stranger, placing the charge in the hand of the smith, "and I pray that by the operation of the grace of God upon your heart your feet may soon be shod with the preparation of the gospel of peace. You carry on more than your mere trade in this workshop, friend; see to it that the record be written by Him who keeps a book of remembrance of them that fear the Lord and think upon his name. What a messenger you might be of love and mercy from the Prince of peace to those who come to talk with you here!"

"They would not come for a sermon, I reckon," said Jeffry, attempting to laugh as he looked round.

"Try it; and the next piece of iron you mould by yonder fire, liken it in your mind to a hard human heart, cast under the softening influence of divine love, and reshaped by the omnipotent Creator for holy and happy uses. Goodnight, friends all, and the Lord be with you."

"Stop, sir," said the smith, stepping after the traveller, and laying his hand on the bridle-rein. "Who are you that talks to Jeffry Hayes in this uncommon way?"

"One who had a message from God unto you, and has delivered it," replied the stranger, as he rode quickly away, leaving the smith gazing after him into the darkness, until the sound of his steps had died away on the night air.

About half an hour afterwards, as Mary Hayes sat knitting by her cottage-fire, she was surprised by the arrival of her husband full two hours before his usual time; and being a person of good sense she uttered no comment, but set his chair, and, while he washed away the marks of his daily toil, prepared supper and brought in a small jug of ale as naturally as if it were his custom to drink it quietly in her company at home. Hayes did not seem to have much appetite, nor disposed to be very communicative; but, after looking at the fire for some time, he suddenly spoke, —

"Mary, have we got a Bible?"

"A Bible? Oh, yes! Don't you remember the big book that mistress gave me when we were married?"

"Ah, to be sure! Get it, — will you? I want to find something in it."

But leaf after leaf was turned over in vain. The Bible to Jeffry Hayes was like a foreign land to one ignorant of geography.

"I can't find it," said he; "can't you, Mary? Something about feet shod with the gospel of peace."

Alas! Mary was not much better informed than her husband, until she remembered that there was a passage about armor in one of the epistles; whereupon, with her knitting-needle to glide before her eyes down the pages verse by verse, she finally settled it triumphantly upon the fifteenth verse of the last chapter in the Epistle to the Ephesians.

"That's it!" said her husband, gratified at the discovery; and, having read the verse, he read the chapter, and afterwards the epistle too.

"Mary," said he again, after another revery, "there is to be a fight between young Moss of the dell and Will Crofts of our village."

"A fight!" exclaimed Mary; for such an announcement was the furthest from her busy thoughts at that moment; "and are you to be in the thick of it as usual?"

"I promised to be with them, and see fair play, and I must keep my word."

"Then what have you to do with the Bible and the gospel of peace?" asked Mary, quickly.

"I want to see if we can't have fair

16

play, and yet no fighting," said Hayes, thoughtfully, "and I shall search here for a way till I find one."

Mary marvelled greatly, as her husband regularly came home every evening to pursue that search, and she remarked how much fewer were the profane or angry expressions which now mingled with his conversation.

The day fixed for the fight at last arrived, and Jeffry Hayes, standing between the waiting combatants, and surrounded by an eager ring of village gazers, took a hand of each. "Well," said he, looking from one to the other, "which of you is the most like Cain? Which is prepared to show himself a murderer?"

The young men, surprised and sullen,

sought to withdraw their hands from the blacksmith's grasp.

"Look you, my friends," said he; " I promised to come here to see fair play, and, as I helped on the quarrel in the beginning, it is fit that I should see the end of it. I tell you both that fair play is to forgive one another, and the bravest of you is he who dares to forgive first. Come down, now, and talk it over with me at the forge, and I'll prove to you that this is the right way of thinking. Good-morrow, friends; there will be no fighting, I promise you."

"You are making fools of us, smith," said one of the youths, angrily.

"No, no; you did that for yourselves when you quarrelled about nothing, and I want to see you wise men again."

"What a queer end to a fight!" exclaimed the disappointed villagers, as Jeffry Hayes marched triumphantly off the ground, with a stout, sheepish-looking youth on either side. "Only to think of great Jeffry Hayes turning peacemaker; it's as good as a fight to see it,—so we haven't altogether lost our time."

Some four or five years afterward a passing visitor at the Hall walked through that village with the squire. The evening was drawing on, and the blacksmith's forge was becoming conspicuous in the deepening twilight. "You must just look in here for a moment before we return," said the squire, "for I am proud of our village smith: he is a tamed lion; once the most fiery, quarrelsome fellow in the county, and a violent politician, too, with a frame strong enough to enforce any argument and carry any bad majority; but now the quietest, soberest, and most Christian man I know of."

Here they reached the forge, and were respectfully greeted by Jeffry Hayes.

"My friend," said the visitor, after looking at him for a few moments, as if endeavoring to recall some recollections of the past, "if I mistake not, you once shod my horse on a dark winter evening, and I" —

"Sir, if I mistake not," exclaimed Jeffry, with a glow of pleasure on his face, after an equally searching look at the stranger's countenance, and an attentive ear to his voice, "if I mistake not, you are the King's messenger who bore the pardon for guilty rebels on that night. It was 'a word in season,' sir, and I have proved how good it was. It led me to turn from darkness to light, and changed the village firebrand into a meeker, happier man. And now, by God's mercy, the rebel blacksmith seeks to be a King's messenger himself."

www.ingramcontent.com/pod-product-compliance
Lightning Source LLC
Chambersburg PA
CBHW051556030726
47592CB00001B/311